I0471241

OBAMACARE FUNDING: OMG! DEMS THINK THEY ARE BIGGEST WINNERS, BUT ACTUALLY MAY BE THE DUMBEST FOOLS!

The Obamacare mess is sort of like a high stakes poker game. But, I think the real hole cards are what the voting public is going to do in the 2014 and 2016 elections.

The Dems are praying for a government shutdown that will definitely give them an advantage going into these elections. And on the other hand there is a small group of gung-ho arch-conservatives that could care less if the government gets shut down in their effort to stop this funding.

Sure, everyone knows this small group of conservatives won't be able to stop this funding. Myself, I think their failure is a blessing in disguise. I think the worse possible nightmare may happen to the Dems if they go ahead and put Obamacare in effect at this time.

There is no risk to wait a year. It is already the law and nothing would really change, plus it would give them another year to get all of their ducks in line. And they would probably hold on to the senate.

That said, they are risking everything because the cold hard fact is the economy can't swallow Obamacare and unimaginable things are going to happen. The forty hour work week may be history. People may start losing jobs like crazy causing the dole to explode. And the tax base may start drastically dwindling.

With all that going on the voters may finally see the light and give the hated republicans their chance to shine in 2014 and 2016. If nothing else, this will give the Dems something to think about.
SIRMANS LOG: 24 SEPTEMBER 2013, 1948 HOURS

ANY DRASTIC USA CUTS IN

SPENDING WILL BE LIKE COMMITTING INSTANT ECONOMIC DEATH!

All of these decent good intention people that is hollering and demanding drastic cuts in government spending are economically ignorant.

To drastic cut spending in a welfare state before first abolishing the "Minimum wage law" is committing economic suicide. Drastic cuts in spending will only create a smaller welfare state pie, and it still will have to be divided as before with even more mouths to feed.

Starting with the "New deal" the shallow minded liberals brought us to this point, but, we all are guilty of taking the course of least resistance. Now, the end result is we are past the stage of no return. In my view there is no stopping it, the USA and world economy will soon collapse no matter what man does.

The USA's best bet is to abolish the "Minimum wage law." And pray that unleashing a true genuine free market place won't be too late to allow freedom to survive and not be lost for another ten thousand years.

From a nature point of view, the "Boom and bust cycle is the same as the "Life and death" cycle; at some point its rotation cycle will not be denied.
SIRMANS LOG: 23 SEPTEMBER 2013, 1851 HOURS

WILL INDIVIDUAL FREEDOM BE WIPED OFF THE FACE OF THE EARTH FOREVER?

I don't think so, but many people do think I preach doom and gloom as a writer. Concerning all of this Obamacare mess, I heard a guy on TV make a profound statement. He said we are not going to be able to unscramble this egg, which I totally agree.

I believe Obamacare is the last straw that is going to break the USA economy's back by exploding the dole.

So, I am hoping when all of the smoke and fog clears A black knight will ride in on a white horse and slay the evil "Minimum wage law" villain, then a true genuine "Free market place" can freely raise up like a Phoenix and save individual freedom from being lost forever.
SIRMANS LOG: 20 SEPTEMBER 2013, 1141 HOURS

AMERICANS BELIEVE IN SLAVERY AND DON'T REALIZE IT!

This morning I heard a man on TV say he believe that food was a right and also medical care was a right. Now, hardly anyone saw anything wrong with that type of thinking, because practically all liberals and 90 percent of the American population agree with him.

But, I'll tell you with that type of thinking on a wide enough scale there is no way the USA can be saved. Let me interpret what he said. Wisdom wise he and others has no idea what that type of thinking really means or equals to.

Thinking like that equals to saying there is "Something for nothing in life." And believing anyone is entitle to free medical care is the same as believing in slavery. How else is anyone entitle to free medical care unless there are slaves to provide it.

The doctors, nurses, and medical care workers would all have to be slaves for anyone to be entitle to free medical care. That said, I will say again for the umpteenth time, only "Abolishing the minimum wage law" can save this great nation.

Doing that will untie what made this a great exceptional nation in the first place, a true genuine "Free market place."

Oh! OK! Now I see! We are entitle to free food and medical care because the government is our daddy provider and should pay for it, (SMDH) shake my damn head. Sure, that-a-work until there are more free loaders riding in the wagon than pushing the wagon.

After all everyone loves riding a free horse or a grave train.
SIRMANS LOG: 19 SEPTEMBER 2013, 1043 HOURS

A SWEET LITTLE SUGAR PIE!
Folks, I take no pleasure in taking a stand on something I know 98 percent of the American people disagree with me on. But, I am driven by some unknown force to sound the distress call to survive.

We are human being and we all are controlled by self-interest and emotions. That mean in the grand theme of things it won't really matter what the democrats do, what the republicans do, or what tax changes are made. The USA economy is still going to totally collapse. That is because what got us here in the first place self-interest and emotions haven't changed.

Our survival must be turned over to a system that has never failed, that system will do what must be done to assure our survival, and that system is a true free market place. But, there is only one thing blocking our way to that true free market place. And that one thing is a sweet little sugar pie.

Her name is "Minimum wage law." She has a spell on all of us. Myself, I plead abstinent.
SIRMANS LOG: 13 SEPTEMBER 2013, 2213 HOURS

WORLD POWER CHESS GAME, NEXT MOVE!

Suppose there are world leaders that read my work and don't believe the USA will ever abolish the minimum wage law. That means the USA economy cannot be saved and will soon totally collapse.

You can't stay a great military power without being backed by a great economy, period. Not everyone ignores the great supernatural wisdom of this great writer.

It won't be pretty but abolishing the

minimum wage law will allow a true free market place to kick in and save the USA. Trust me; nothing else can save the USA from total doom no matter what the egg heads and learned economist tell you.

A true free market place has never failed in the history of man kind. SIRMANS LOG: 12 SEPTEMBER 2013, 1039 HOURS

GUARANTEED WEIGHT CONTROL!

I know that weight control is 90 percent mental. And I do believe in positive thinking to change behavior. So, I repeat to myself over and over at least 50 times or more every day this quote: "I love my slim and healthy body." It has certainly helped me a lot but not overnight it took some time to work.
SIRMANS LOG: 10 SEPTEMBER 2013, 1044 HOURS

RACISM VERSUS SUBJECTIVITY IN AMERICA!

Let's just get real here, reality and

subjectivity is two different things. However, some people do have a problem distinguishing between objectivity and subjectivity. We in America are ruled by law not by man or his subjective emotions, thank God.

We in America probably have more different races and religions than any nation on earth, yet have less friction. The reality is no one race in America is treated extra special, especially the African American race. Now, who and why would anyone advocate that African Americans are treated extra special.

I just don't believe the facts backs up anything of the sort, I suspect there may be a feeling of superiority subjectivity at play here.
SIRMANS LOG: 09 SEPTEMBER 2013, 1545 HOURS

DYING USA ECONOMY STILL ECONOMIC ENGINE FOR THE WORLD!

Minimum wage, minimum wage, minimum wage equal Ignorance,

ignorance ignorance! Almost everyone is focused only on the minimum wage to make more money. But, it is not the minimum wage that is financially killing everyone; it is the buying power and the cost of living that is killing everyone.

It is dumb and one-dimensional economically in a free market place to force any amount of wage or price control on the people. Why do you think most of the world is poor and will always be poor, they won't allow a true free market place?

A forced minimum wage on the people more than anything else has destroyed the USA economy, our nuclear and extended family system, and our moral code. Yet, even a crippled and dying USA economy still has enough free market place capacity left to remain the economic engine of the world.

The Dragons, little Dragons and all other economies of the world would sputter to a screeching halt if the huge USA lifeblood market dried up. So, instead of always focusing only on more money to live on, people need to know the real reason why the cost of everything you buy is too high. Duh.

Water is free; it's the processing and piping you pay for. Whatever happened to being able to live off the land?

Free Market, free market, free market, what a joke. When government forces any wage or price control (minimum wage) on the people there is nothing free about that. Within the next two years we are going to pay an awesome price for this if we survive at all as a nation.

Sure, the intentions on having a minimum wage are good, but the way to hell is paved with good intentions. Economically wise it is insane and we can't and won't survive with a minimum wage in place, period. SIRMANS LOG: 04 SEPTEMBER 2013, 1053 HOURS

SLAVE FIELD-HAND MENTALITY

GRIP STILL BINDING.

Wake up African American political and spiritual leadership, grow up and take responsibility, you are not a field-hand anymore. You are now up on the hill in the big house now.

You must now take on the responsibility of running the place. You must now create your own jobs and means of making a living. You must set a budget and make sure the family gets fed, whereas as a field-hand all you had to do was work and obey orders.

You are now the master of your own destiny now, if you don't do it yourself it may not get done, you are not a dependent anymore. Fast forward to the year of our Lord 2013, the African American race has a serious problem.

People are afraid of African American men, especially young black males. Reality is reality and it is what it is. There is an old saying: You can't make other people change, but, you can change yourself then the world around you will change.

If you don't believe that here is an example: Stress: If anyone on your job or anywhere causes you a lot of stress, just repeat this quote to yourself over and over as long as necessary, "I can wish all people goodwill no matter how they treat me," then the stress will vanish. This is only a tool and not for every situation.

Black males are stereotyped as dangerous and violent prone. A stereotype can be overcome and gotten rid of. You get rid of a stereotype by proving over time that it is no longer true. But, that can't be done until one accepts responsibility and stop blaming circumstance and the system.

There is no excuse why Africans Americans can't obey the law and behave as good as any race, period. Any winning coach will tell you, you are going to get some bad calls but you focus even harder on your game plan.

Sure, as a minority the system may not give a black man a break and in some cases may even be unfair, still, there is no excuse why African Americans can't obey the law and behave as good as any Race.

I'm over seventy and from the Deep South and I remember before the welfare state destroyed the black family, no one feared a black man walking into a country store.

Many years ago in the USA the Japanese were stereotyped as the junk and trinket merchants. But, through hard work and quality control they proved that they could produce as good a product as any nation. Today no one doubts the quality of Japanese products.

African American political and spiritual leaders need to believe and prove that the African American race can behave and obey the law as good as any race, period. Like me or hate me, still, how can any self-respecting responsible

African American disagree with me on this, (SMH) shake my head.

The black community itself suffers more than anyone from all of this violence. Do-for-myself responsible hands need to grab the MLK, Jr. baton and take it into the home stretch to full equality and justice.

And, tell the liberals we don't need your pity or patronizing services any longer
SIRMANS LOG: 27 AUGUSTA 2013, 2135 HOURS

IS MASS STARVATION AND SUFFERING AHEAD FOR THE USA?
Almost everyone thinks that I'm really the nut and stupid one for constantly wanting to eliminate the minimum wage law entirely.

Well, I know and anyone with a deep understanding of economics knows that the USA and world economy may soon collapse. When this happens the minimum wage law will disappear and there may be chaos, mass suffering, and starvation if we survive at all.

So, all I'm saying is why go through all of that un-necessarily
when voluntarily abolishing the minimum wage law will prevent it. One way or another the minimum wage will go the way of the great Auk, (SMDH) shake my damn head.

Obamacare is simply the straw that is going to break the camels back.
SIRMANS LOG: 25 AUGUST 2013, 1834 HOURS

"OUR FALSE GOD OF DOOM!"
Just like the big enemy armored divisions of World War II ran on ball bearings our liberal created welfare state runs on the minimum wage law. In sheer economic terms the minimum wage law is "Our false God of doom."

It is impossible to save the USA or western civilization unless the minimum wage law death grip is broken. The laws of economics

demands that the minimum wage law must go or the USA bites the dust.
SIRMANS LOG: 24 AUGUST 2013, 0625 HOURS

YOUNG CHILDHOOD SEXUAL ABUSE!

This doesn't belong here and I shouldn't be saying it anyway, it concerns childhood sexual abuse. My view is very simple; if you do the crime you do the time or pay with your life, period.

The good book says flee from temptation, which a wise man will heed to. Contrary to what most people may think there are abnormal forces out there that are almost impossible to resist unless one flees.

Example: A young child sexually abused may become obsessed with sex and become armed with the power of sexual projection. The child grows up but the abnormal power of projection remains. Now, if someone with this abnormal power focuses it on you for whatever reason, your best bet is to get the hell out of Dodge and fast.

Enough said, something like this is never talked about anyway. Ignorance is bliss and just thank God nothing like this has ever happened to you. Believe it or not there are forces out there that only a strong moral and spiritual person can withstand, it's rare, but, it does exist.

"The human mind is a very powerful thing".
SIRMANS LOG: 20 AUGUST 2013, 1138 HOURS

IS A GOVERNMENT SHUTDOWN INEVITABLE?
Right or wrong the republicans are stupid if they force any issue that will end in a government shut down. It will be a lose, lose situation for republicans any way you look at it.

The liberals including the vast majority of the mass media in my view will have a blaming field day. Besides, after the first huge public outcry the vast majority of the republicans will head for the tall grass or high tail it out of Dodge anyway. And even if the republicans could win some kind of hollow victory, very little would change, we still remain a welfare state.

This welfare state is on automatic pilot and nothing or nobody is going to stop it unless its fuel is cut off. Sure, a collapse will stop it but no sane reasonable person wants that, cutting spending won't stop it that will only get the republicans out of office.

Believe it or not, the fuel that propels this whole welfare state is the minimum wage. It is impossible for the USA to survive as a welfare state. But, it is also impossible for the USA to get out of being a welfare state when government sets any wage or price control.

You can't have a true free market economy when government sets any amount of wage or price control. The minimum wage law allows government to inflate the currency so it can keep its power as a super social and family provider.

But, government should never be a social and family provider in the first place because that destroys the nuclear and extended family system. Without a strong nuclear family system it is impossible to remain a free people after four generations.

If the republicans really want to go to the mat for something do something sane like abolishing the minimum wage law entirely. That is the only thing that can save our great nation. yeah! I know! I stand alone on knowing this fact.
SIRMANS LOG: 4 AUGUST 2013, 2210 HOURS

A Freddie L. Sirmans quote:
Abolishing the minimum wage law will drain the swamp. The swamp is where the welfare state beast lives. The swamp is where all of the anti-survival morality snatchers are coming from.
 The anti-survival morality snatchers

are slowly taking over all of our souls.

TRIVIA NOTE:
Holiday Street in Valdosta, GA. is located within a few yards of where the home was located of the famous western gun fighter "Doc Holiday." It was where he lived as a teenager before going to dental school and heading out west.

WISDOM NOTE:
No one can achieve the great supernatural wisdom that I have without paying an awesome price to survive, and in my case it has been a knockout drag out mentally battle to survive practically all of my life. Still, I have no monopoly on pain or struggle.

PASSING THOUGHT:
If abolishing the minimum wage law is not going to be taken seriously by the USA I'm beginning to suspect the Mayan calendar may not be very far off the mark after all.

FOREWORDS:
Economic ignorance galore abounds,

that's what it is: This caller made a profound statement on TV this morning, his view was that the tax payers were the source of all government funding. Wow! This guy was on to something and he knew more than most, but, he was wrong. Okay, let's do a walk through.

Government funding does come from the tax payers, but, where do the tax payers get their money? All tax payers get their money from their employers or some type of business transaction, period. It goes further; still we haven't arrived at the source of all government funding.

The real source is what gives in my view the shallow minded liberals a problem and is the reason liberals with total power is so dangerous to freedom and democracy. The true answer is: All government funding comes from some type of private business profit.

It is all about profit, profit, and more profit and that can come only from private enterprise. The government can only tax profit or the result of some type of profit, otherwise it cannot survive, period.

In general the shallow minded liberals hate the word profit and too a lesser degree hate business people. The welfare state is the reason the man or woman on the street has no concept of the true role of profit except personally having cash in hand.

You can't get blood out of a turnip and government can't tax where no profit is made. Look at Detroit and California all bastions of liberalism. Unless the minimum wage law is abolished to break the liberal death choke hold on the throat of America that will be the picture of the whole country. God save America!

Liberals are who they are and they love America as much as I do even if I do think they are shallow. It is not entirely the liberals fault, it is the system that got us in our dire situation and only the system can save us, that is why the minimum wage law must be abolished entirely.

Everyone wants to make more money and no one want to make less when we can't make ends meet as it is. But, my great supernatural wisdom know abolishing the minimum wage law is the only way out for the USA to survive, period.

If not for the minimum wage law the cost of living for the poor and everyone would drop so they could pay their own food and doctor bills especially with nuclear family help. But, then the government would lose its God like power as a super provider.

The minimum wage law is blocking everything we buy from dropping down where the poor can pay out of pocket like a free market has always worked before the "New deal." It is the buying power of money that truly matters, not some inflated worthless high number. SIRMANS LOG: 24 JUNE 2013, 1123 HOURS

USA CRIMINAL JUSTICE SYSTEM IS

NOT PERFECT BUT STILL THE WORLDS BEST.

Let me try to shine some light on this. In the USA we have an adversarial criminal justice system which is not perfect but overall still the fairest known to man.

The prosecutor tries everything it can to win the case and on the other hand the Defense tries everything it can to prevent losing the case. Well. Most of the time somewhere in the middle justice will be realized but not always.

The system is not about emotions, right or wrong, or feelings because then justice would always be one-sided and never balanced. However, Joe six-pack and most laymen's believe that if you commit the first wrong and a tragedy result the blame is on you, period.

Sure, Christianity allows mercy and forgiveness, but, when you set a tragedy in motion you can't expect a pat on the back and hero worshiping unless racial bias is involved.

The biggest loser in this whole thing could end up being the Democratic Party. That is because if the blacks stay pissed-off enough they may stay home during the mid term election next year.

This is a dire survival situation in the eyes of most blacks; yet, I for one believe there is some un-necessary stoking of this highly emotional matter. Cooler and calmer heads is what's needed, instead of a lot of flamboyant rhetoric that fans the flames.
SIRMANS LOG: Updated 17 JULY 2013, 1103 HOURS.

OK:
I have commented on this tragedy, so I might as well go whole hog and say what I really feel about the overall African American situation. But, this is an emotional charged issue and I know that truth and reasoning's won't win me a popularity contest.

Sure, there is racialism in America, always has been and always will be.

However, racialism may be an obstacle but that is not what is holding African Americans back or down, especially in this day and time. Before the welfare state came along African Americans faced slavery and a far harsher climate than today, Yet, still owned far more.

I'm going to cut right through the chase and strike right at the heart of the African American community problem. I think as a rule African Americans still has a slavery dependency mentality and don't feel entirely responsible for their own survival as a race.

African Americans are stereotyped as violent prone, criminal prone, likely to lower property values, and bring social baggage in most cases. Whoa, anybody thinking that must be a racialist, maybe or maybe not.

What is never said or admitted is every stereotype has a truth foundation. And you can't dismiss a stereotype by ignoring it and making excuses for bad behavior. When bad behavior is excused and ignored it will reflect on the entire race. And it is not facing reality to think otherwise.

Yet, ignoring that fact is typical liberal behavior. By the African American leadership not taking responsibility for our own behavior as a race causes us all to suffer the consequences of being stereotyped in a bad way. Jealousy, envy, sibling rivalry, and a host of negative emotions come along with having a dependent mentality.

Whereas one with an independent mentality tends to soars above the negative stuff, and will accept total responsibility for himself, his race, and his country. As to jobs, the white man is expected to supply all of the jobs. There are plenty of African Americans with plenty of money, why shouldn't blacks as race be expected to supply more of their own jobs to their community.

I could go on and on but I think I made my point; we need to get a grip and feel totally responsible. I don't have the answer but I do know before the welfare state no one feared black men. Before you can solve a problem you first must admit you have a problem.

I say the African American community has a problem facing up to the truth. And I think it boils down to taking total responsibility for one's own survival. The surest way to cure dependency is to have the props and crutches taken away, but that can't happen as long as we have a welfare state.

Denying truth is the same as denying reality. And that is exactly what African Americans leadership and spiritual leaders have been doing for years concerning black crime. I have no power to stop bad behavior or crime, but, you can bet your bottom dollar that I will never condone it or make excuses for it no matter who does it.

Folks, I have no power to change anything, I'm just thankful I can still write and say what I believe. God Bless America.

SIRMANS LOG: 19 JULY 2013, 2234 HOURS

USA SUPREME COURT CONFIRMS THE VALIDITY OF MY WRITING!

For over twenty years even I at times have questioned the worth or validity of my writing. But, not anymore, since the supreme court all but struck down the defensive marriage act on 26 JUNE 2013.

Folks, it's over for the great USA and western civilization. And the really sad part is very few people even realize it. It is very simple, there has never been and never will be a civilization that last over 80-100 years without a strong nuclear and extended family system, period.

What the Supreme Court did was drive the final nail in the coffin of a strong nuclear and extended family system. Now! Let me tell you why I know I am right beyond a shadow of a doubt. The nuclear and extended family system has kept civilization intact for over

6,000 years.

That was until the early 1930's in the USA when a group of liberal geniuses did something that had never been done in the history of mankind; they seized the family provider role for the government itself. Wow! Wham! Bam! Armed with the "New deal" programs the government became "The great white father" and sugar daddy.

What the shallow minded liberals failed to realize and still haven't to this day is understand that the provider role is the Key to civilization and its survival. What is taught and instilled in the young is what maintains and keep society stable and intact.

Norms and traditions must be instilled for safety and survival because they are based on past trial and experience. This must duty for over 6,000 years was tasked to the provider of each nuclear family unit. The nuclear family provider is the only one with the power and authority to make sure this must duty is carried out.

The family provider should have the physical, financial, and moral capacity to perform this duty thereby safeguarding and maintaining a healthy civilized society. Well, we all know what happened; the USA government seized the provider role for itself and got drunk on power. So, you can forget about it yielding even one inch, ever.

Sure, it provided food and shelter, but failed to enforce any other must provider duty. Failure by the government as the provider to make sure norms and traditions were instilled in the young meant death to the USA four generations into the future. And sure enough here we are around four generations later with almost everything ass backward.

Same sex marriage and mass killing in the womb seem to be the norm today which would have been insane at the time, and now sound judgment is something you find in the history books. And, you are going to convince me that this nation can survive, @#%$*%$#, I love you too!

But, due to my great supernatural wisdom I see one last chance for the USA to survive. And we can still survive with freedom still intact provided we as a nation abolish the minimum wage law; otherwise we go the way of the great Auk.
SIRMANS LOG: 27 JUNE 2013, 1255 HOURS

THE FULL DESTRUCTIVE FORCE OF OBAMACARE IS FIXING TO HIT!

All seems to be calm and quiet on the home front; they say the housing market is booming. So, what is there to fear? It is almost always quiet before the storm. I'll tell you what's lurking out there, the full destructive force of Obamacare is about to hit.

I also predict that the dole is likely to explode and then all hell is going to break lose when Obamacare fully hit.

So, my advice is brace yourself the s... is about to hit the fan. There is already a mad rush by businesses to stay below 50 employees and keep the work week below 30 hours.

There is already over 48,000.000 million on the food stamps dole alone, plus, we are already $17,000.000.000.000 trillion in debt and borrowing 40 cents of every dollar the government spends. Now, you are going to convince me otherwise that at some point the USA government is not going to prostitute our sovereignty away?#@%!, spare me.

So, in a few more months when Obamacare fully kicks in it may be Katie bar the door. In my view everything Washington enacts now if it's not to abolish the minimum wage law is going to be an exercise in futility.

I think the USA is at a do or die stage, and dealing with the root problem first is a must and anything else is a waste of precious time. I see the USA destructive root problem as government's seized role of being a "Social and family provider."

The USA government as a social and family provider has ran it course which is a role it should never have gotten into in the first place. The "New deal" seized the provider role from the nuclear and extended family system where it had been for over 6,000 years.

Until the USA government gets the hell out of the social and family provider business the USA cannot and will not survive, period. It's just that simple, either the USA government jettisons its social and family provider role or we go the way of the great auk, there is no way to get around that fact.

The only way to save the USA before a total economic collapse results from Obamacare and an exploding dole is to abolish the minimum wage law now. I know in today's climate very few has the wisdom or depth to see how abolishing the minimum wage would save the USA economy.

That is why I really don't see the minimum wage ever being abolishing voluntarily, still, I must never stop pounding for it. Even if no one else do I know only abolishing the minimum wage can safely bleed off the pressure and save the USA economy, because there is no doubt in my mind it is fixing to blow or collapse.

Sure, before the "New deal" there was much suffering especially the elderly. But, the tried and true nuclear and extended family provider system has proven itself for over 6,000 years, it's not perfect, but it works and doesn't destroy morality. Plus, the nuclear and extended family provider system is never a threat to bring down the whole system and send us all back to the Stone Age.

Whereas, the "New deal" has given us this tax hungry welfare state socialist beast. This beast has all but destroyed the nuclear family, family values, and sunk our morals to the point that we have same sex marriage and mass killing of the unborn in the womb. And even worse, very few USA citizens even care or give a damn, to them that's just the new norm.

Yet, someone like me is seen as a nut case and a throw back that should be ignored or locked away some where. With all of this going on the USA cannot and will not survive unless the minimum wage is abolished to bring back some sanity.

We are just too far gone into this swamp of value rot and moral decay, only a physical barrier like abolishing the minimum wage can save us now. Man is control by logic and self-interest which means the way to hell is paved with good intentions.

"Be still God will fight your battle," but, in this case, abolish the "Minimum wage law, then be still, and the invisible hand which is nature's supreme law of "Natural selection" will save the USA economy and western civilization, too.

SIRMANS LOG: 9 MAY 2013, 1243 HOURS.

FREDDIE L SIRMANS SR. SHORT BASIC LECTURE ON UNDERSTANDING AN ECONOMY!

Am I dumb, ignorant, or just plain stupid, I'm sure many people think so because I keep harping on abolishing the minimum wage law. What if I am a kook or loon, still, that don't prove me wrong. Sure, when you look at it on an individual or personal basis obviously no one want to make less income.

On the surface a minimum wage seems like a good thing just like most things that have create this welfare state beast we have. In my view even most learned economist doesn't really understand how a free market place economy is supposed to work.

The real truth is it is nature's supreme law of "Natural selection" that really controls everything in nature including the working of an economy. And anyone that doesn't understand nature can never understand an economy.

The first understanding is listening to the words, it says natural selection and free market, force is nowhere to be found. So, that means the first rule to understanding an economy is force will never get you the most production out of an economy.

A minimum wage law is the use of force and it slows production and may even bring growth to a halt. Without a minimum wage law many more businesses could start small and grow into giants.

Many big business men will tell you

that if they had to start today they could never have gotten off the ground. All a minimum wage really does in terms of progress is give more power to the government to control private property.

The minimum wage law keeps money inflated for government to have enough to pay one group not to work and tax the other group to death which allows government to stay drunk on power. Right now the government have taken over and own far more private property than a hundred years ago and will probably end up owning it all.

Another reason why people don't understand economics is first you have to understand human nature to understand economics. A good example is "Greed," almost everyone thinks greed is a bad thing for an economy, wrong; nothing could be further from the truth.

Nothing can replace greed. There is no greater energy packed motivating force in our entire human makeup than greed. Greed is something that must be harnessed, but, never smothered out or severely restricted if you want a successful economy.

There has never been a rich and prosperous nation without a lot of greedy people to make it happen. Greed can be compared to electricity, very dangerous, but very little progress can be made in terms of wealth without it.

A free market place with free competition is the perfect way to harness greed without smothering or snuffing it out, like the communist or socialist. There never have been and never will be a rich and prosperous pure communist or socialist state.

The USA is no longer even close to having a genuine free market place. A genuine free market economic have never in history failed to produce far more than that nation can use in almost everything.

Yet those in power that love power and control may tolerate the free market but still hate it. The reason power hungry leaders don't like the free market is kin or no kin if you don't produce you are gone.

In closing I will add this little nugget:

To create great wealth one must be willing to take great risk. But, no one is going to take great risk without a fair chance for a great reward, period. Why work extra hard and produce more when non producers get an equal share that is where the great USA seems to be headed.

I hope my short economic lecture have been helpful to you in some way. I am a creative self-made writer; most of what you get is my own original thinking.   SIRMANS LOG: 16 MAY 2013, 2056 HOURS.

EXTRA INPUT: 23 MAY 2013, 0135 HOURS.
Let me say this to around 95 percent of the USA population that strongly disagrees with me and my views on abolishing the minimum wage law, there is a very important question that you have failed to ask.

That question is: what are you and the

country going to do when the USA government doesn't have the money and can't borrow it to pay its bills. Huh! That's the problem! Over 95 percent of the USA population have never imagined let alone asked a question of the sort.

Almost everyone seems to think of the USA government as some kind of omnipotent money sow that we can suck on her tits forever. But, nothing could be further from the truth. There never has been and never will be a government that doesn't go broke at some point.

Even worse, the USA has a social and family provider government that amounts to a socialist welfare state. The USA economy not only can collapse it will collapse as soon as Obamacare fully kicks in in a few months.

No matter what the learned economist and egg heads may tell you, self-made writer little ole me is telling you the

USA economy is on the brink and when Obamacare fully kicks in it will collapse.

Sure, probably no one is going to believe me, no problem, we all will know in a few months if the USA economy can swallow Obamacare and survive.

Of course, any suspense could be avoided if the USA just took the bull by the horns and abolished the minimum wage law which would no doubt save the USA economy.

THE "NEW DEAL" CURSE!

Family discipline is the extremely important ingredient that has been missing in the USA ever since the "New deal" seized the provider role from the nuclear and extended family system.

The nuclear and extended family system is where the provider role stayed for over 6,000 years until the "New deal" seized it in the name of Mr. Do-gooder.

However, being a provider is much, much more than just providing food and shelter. The provider is the only one with the power and control to enforce and maintain discipline and instill it in the young.

For any society to survive over four generations the provider must safeguard norms and traditions and make sure they are instilled in the young.

So, when the shallow minded liberals armed with the "New deal" seized the provider role for itself it failed to take on provider duties and responsibilities that have been carried out for over 6,000 years. And the liberals are still doing this crime against USA society.

This shallow senseless liberal destruction has devastated and all but destroyed the African American community in the USA and the cancer is well on it's way to destroying all of USA society.

Now, here we are in the year of our Lord two thousand thirteenth year with 95 percent of the USA population left with the survival instinct of a 10 year old.

We are at death door in terms of human survival with all of our eggs in one basket. We solely depend on a bloated wobbly kneed socialist welfare state beast that could totally collapse any moment and send civilization all the way back to the stone age.

No society can survive without a strong nuclear and extended family system, a strong moral and spiritual code in place, and adequate emergency backup bartering capacity with many small farmers and home gardeners.

Those were the survival tools that allowed western civilization to survive the great depression, which today is practically nonexistent. The stone age may be our only destination.

That is because nature's law of "Boom and Bust" is like the life and death cycle there can be no long term survival unless it is carried out. Yet, here I am with an almost super natural strong survival instinct and I'm seen as a nut, kook, loon, or some other reject or hater.

I plead and I plead for sanity like abolishing the minimum wage law which I know will save my beloved homeland, the only home I know.

Having this great wisdom and super strong survival instinct is like a curse to me; I can dissect an economy and see straight to the core of most things when so many just don't get it. God, I ask in your name bless the USA home of the brave and the free.

MAN HAS NEVER SET FOOT ON THE MOON? SIRMANS LOG: 02 JUNE 2013, 1750 HOURS

Awhile back I wrote an article that I was 99.9 percent sure that man landed on the moon but I still can't get past that .1 percent. It's not that I am dumb or stupid; I understand electronics and modern science.

Right out of high school back in 1962 I took a six month course in radio and TV repair. Back then we studied mainly the super heterodyne receiver and vacuum tubes. The transistor was just coming into play the same as the cathode ray vacuum tube which was the early TV.

We also learned about waves and frequencies. So, on my part it just doesn't make any sense for me to doubt that they landed on the moon. When I wrote the first article on this subject a guy asked me in a comment did I have any proof that they didn't land on the moon, and I said "No."

In replying I told him it was just a gut feeling, and that is still what haunts me on how I feel about the whole matter. There is something about this whole thing that logical just doesn't add up in my way of thinking. I feel something is wrong somewhere.

Even if they did land, maybe they found something up there (UFO) that they are not telling. I have a fair understanding of human nature, and there have never been a case where man opened up a new frontier and didn't exploit it in some way.

Like I said, maybe there is a big hidden mystery that maybe it's better the public never knows about. I don't have any inside information, just a raw gut feeling. This article may be the smoking gun or the last straw that I really am a nut, kook, or loon, who cares, some already believe that anyway.

However, I am not entirely alone doubting that man landed on the moon, 10 percent of the USA population is Doubting Thomas's on this. God bless America.

THE USA LAST SUPPER!
SIRMANS LOG: 9 JUNE 2013, 1954 HOURS

Anyone that can stomach reading my work knows that I have a super mind agree or not. So, I have decided to draw a picture and explain what happened to the great USA. I think it boils down to two word "Sound judgment."

Starting with me, probably three percent or less of the USA population agree or truly understand my way of thinking. The vast majority think my writing is some kind of nineteenth century throwback. And they are mostly right, a hundred years ago about ninety five percent of the USA population would have agreed with my way of thinking.

Back then same sex marriage and mass killing in the womb would have been beyond everyone's imagination. Now, ninety five percent or more of the USA population see that as normal. The USA is about evenly split down the middle in terms of voting.

The masses of government dependents see the republicans as the enemy and believe they would like to take away their livelihood. The other half believes the democrats are going to tax and spend the USA out of existence. But, I believe like one politician said: "There is not a dime worth of difference between the two parties."

Sure, there are minor differences in terms of appointing judges but neither party is going to serious stop the growth of government. Overall the Dems and liberals are the reason the USA is in the dire situation it is today. In my view Dems and liberals are just plain shallow, but, super aggressive and will not let morality, country, or anything stand in the way of them grabbing and taking power.

On the other hand the Republican Party has become almost as liberal as the democrat party. I feel the conservatives ought to just flat out take it over. Even conservatives don't agree with my out dated thinking, still I think they are the only ones that can save the USA from total doom.

The thing is they don't know how. Well, it may already be too late but I am going to tell them how to save the USA. However, I'm sure they won't agree and won't take my advice; still I'm going to pass it on anyway. Remember, I said the Key words were "Sound judgment." The Dems and liberals own the thinking and shaping of young minds in the USA.

For over 6,000 years up until the "New deal" the nuclear and extended family system was the primary shaper of young minds, but, not anymore. To a great extent in most situations now the primary shaper of young minds is liberal TV and the liberal school systems. Very few homes are instilling traditional conservative's norms and values.

Almost everything the young comes in contact with now-a-days is liberal. So, of course the young when they mature will not have a conservative foundation to return to like children of old. "Sound judgment" which is everything to keep and maintain a civil society will soon be nowhere to be found.

So, my advice to conservatives is follow my advice cold turkey and go for the jugular. No if ands or buts, fight to abolish the minimum wage law now, not tomorrow. With no minimum wage law the government will lose it power to control private property.

With no minimum wage law government would have to give up its provider role which has all but destroyed our nuclear and extended family system. With no minimum wage law manufacturing would return to the USA and everything would be made in America with jobs for all.

With no minimum wage law the economy would balance itself and the poor could pay their own food and medical bills. With no minimum wage law people would make far less money but $5.00 would buy A week's worth of grocery. And I could go on and on what has been proven to work for over 6,000 years before the "New deal."

Plus here are the cold steel facts, if the minimum wage law is not abolished, the USA is not going to survive and that is a guarantee. Before the "New deal" the male nuclear family provider hands on instilled and enforced norms and traditional conservatives values thereby safe guarding our human survival.

Now, unless the government is kicked out of the provider role the USA has the chance of a snowball in hell of surviving. Abolishing the minimum wage will get the ball rolling on saving my beloved homeland.

I believe in a few months when Obamacare fully kicks in it is going to explode the dole and cause the USA economy to crash and burn. I also believe abolishing the minimum wage law is the only way to stop the USA economy from crashing and burning.

Will congress abolish the minimum wage law? NO! Will the USA and western civilization survive? NO! Reason, the boom and bust cycle is a part of nature the same as the life and death cycle.

Abolishing the minimum wage law

would have save us by allowing the bust cycle to complete it normal rotation, but no, the learned economist and egg heads think they can juggle the figures forever, wrong.

Call me a fool or nut as you wish, but without a doubt I know I am right on this. Sure, no one agrees with me on any of this but they will, the hardship and suffering just hasn't taken it toll yet.

EMERGENCY SURVIVAL PLAN FOR AMERICA BEFORE TOTAL DOOM!
For a few years now I have kept up a constant drum beat to get rid of the minimum wage entirely, to rip it up by the root and burn it to never return. Well, almost no one understands that and can't see the logic of my thinking on this.

The thing about the minimum wage that makes it so destructive to a free market capitalism system is the fact that it is socialism to the core. The truth is it gives the government almost absolute power and control over private property and our free enterprise capitalist system of government.

In fact a free market place ceases to exist when any government sets wage control over private property owners. It doesn't matter if it is one penny or one hundred dollars you decide to pay as long as it is your private property, the government should butt out.

That is why practical all taxes should be on real property or something physical. Any time government controls production and distribution of what you can do with your own private property that is flat out socialism no matter how much they say it is free market capitalism.

In fact this whole matter of a minimum wage to me is not so much about wages but the power it gives government to control private property and what one can do with it. This whole big government welfare state spins off government's ability to control private property through a minimum wage.

The ability of government to set any wage is the true reason the growth of government is impossible to stop. I will repeat, if this great nation is to survive the minimum or any government wage control must be eliminated, period.

It is very simple, I understand the inner workings of an economy as well or better than most people. No one no matter how learned can truly understand economic unless they understand its basics which are trade and bartering first.

Trade and bartering kept people alive and has existed long before a currency was invented. It is simple we don't have enough people producing and growing at least some of their own food. Mass hunger and starving is going to be the end result of all this worthless money the government is printing up.

With this welfare state at this late stage and the course we are on it is ridiculous to even consider getting out of debt, just being able to survive as nation should be the first priority. With the course we are on we will continue to become worse off until a total collapse occur, it is simply inevitable.

My logic is with the course we are on it would be nice to plan on getting out of debt but that is a pipe dream. We must first change course and fight to survive at all cost. I guarantee you it is impossible to save this great nation as a welfare state, period. And I don't give a damn what the learned egg heads or anyone else tells you.

I know beyond a shadow of doubt that the welfare state cannot and will not survive, period. Now, it is down to the people having to save themselves and the nation, the government cannot and will not save this great nation.

More tax money and bigger government will just speed up the day of reckoning, which will be more and more worthless money until the whole thing collapse. That is why when I tell you the minimum wage law must go I know what I am talking about.

The elimination of the minimum wage entirely is our only hope of surviving as a free nation. Eliminating the minimum will set the free market place free to work its magic and save this great nation.

Eliminating the minimum wage will break the deadly choke hold big government and the welfare state has on free enterprise and the free market place. Without the minimum wage, it will allow the citizens the freedom to barter and hire each other as maids, handy man service, or whatever to eat and survive.

As it is now with a minimum wage the average citizen can't hire anyone without wage control and mountains of red tape, why bother. The people must be set free of any kind of wage control for this great nation to survive and that is without a doubt, period.

Anyone with an ounce of economic

sense knows that we can't survive much longer with the course we are on. Every day this nation is printing tons of worthless money and with that going on even an idiot should know that soon money won't be worth the paper it is printed on.

Still, this welfare state beast we have is doing it damnest to grow more government and create more dependents, that is insane, and don't belong in the real world of reality. These hoards of people will be left with no ability to survive on their own, and to me that is a crime against nature.

But, I have no power except my pen to try to bring some sanity to bear. Hopefully my advice will be taken and the minimum wage will be eliminated entirely. But, it doesn't end there the poor and disadvantage has to be protected.

They no longer have the nuclear and extended family umbrella that always stood guard until the welfare state took away that survival need. When this welfare state soon collapses they must have a lifeline.

So, when the minimum wage is completely gotten rid of the poor and disadvantaged still must never be completely abandoned. The first order of business is the government must establish government runs commissaries, housing, and clinics and use tokens or script for all who qualify.

This must be done to keep guaranteed government handout money from contaminating and destroying the free market place as it is now. That is another reason why I know this welfare state economy can never be saved.

What is happening with the economy now is like feeding on you starting with the big toe and continuing until there is no means to survive. We are eating our seed corn and drinking our priming water to wash it down; my God it is sheer insanity.

You just simply cannot have a lasting

free market economy with government dumping tons of free unearned money into it. That is like the tax paying citizens paying to drive up the cost of living on themselves.

With the use of tokens, script, of whatever means government free unearned handout spending must be kept separated out of the free market place. That will stop the cost of living from inflating out of control like what is happening now.
SIRMANS LOG: 21 DECEMBER 2012, 1358 HOURS

THE SANDY HOOK ELEMENTARY SCHOOL CHILD KILLING
I try to stay away from making comments on matters like this because it is hard for me to pull punches. But, I just had to say something and I will make it very brief before getting into too much trouble.

All focus is on the economy and everyone seems to be ignoring the inner fabric of this great nation, but,

I'm here to tell you that the liberal's welfare state has almost completely destroyed the nuclear family and eaten away at the very fabric that holds every society together.

Irresponsible parenting is at the head of the list. Behavior is a result of what one has been conditioned to be. You can bend and shape a young sapling but an older tree will break before it will bend.

Every one is doting on the young like it is just a love thing and it never occurs to hardly anyone that a child is suppose to be a responsible future meal ticket and raised accordingly. Almost every religion in the world warns against worshiping self.

One must believe in someone or something bigger than self to keep from becoming a world into him. One will never take his life or the life of others if he has self-restraint for the feelings of others. And that can be taught, there is almost nothing innate about a human being it is all a learned experience.

I hear people complaining all the time about not being able to enjoy a meal at a restaurant or hear a good movie because an unruly 5 or 6 year old is out of control.

If a parent can't or won't control a 5 or 6 year old and repeat 50 times not to do that, that parent in a reverse way is actually teaching disrespect and disobedience. Then at age 15 many of these kids is lost forever, now whose fault is that! How can you expect someone to be responsible when they have never been conditioned to be responsible?

As far as to gun control, the shallow minded liberals with their candy store has all but destroyed this great nation and knows an armed population is the only thing keeping them from making this a European style socialist state.

They want to get rid of all guns so bad they can taste it, and any excuse will do in their eyes. Thank God we have a second amendment standing guard over individual freedom in America.

Let me shut the hell up I have said too much already. PS: I think almost every social ill we have today can be traced to our liberal induced welfare state, period. I'm out of here.
SIRMANS LOG: 17 DECEMBER 2012, 2011 HOURS

A MINIMUM WAGE MUST BE COMPLETELY ELIMINATED, RIPPED UP BY THE ROOT TO NEVER RETURN.
I have tried to forget about my no "Minimum wage" crusade by thinking it will never happen. I have also thought about my continuing to write and why it seems like a waste of my time. But, it is like some invisible force that drives me to plod on, I'm not making hardly any money at writing, yet, like a zombie I keep marching on.

It has been said that many times when destiny selects you for a mission it will separate you from the crowd and make you a loner. I have no monopoly on one who has experienced a lot of pain and suffering, but I believe I have had more than my fair share.

So many things that the average person takes for granted have been mentally shut off to me, even if it's just in my mind it is still just as real to me. And almost as long as I can remember it has been that way. I don't think it is possible to become a saint without experiencing great pain and suffering. The movie "The Bells of Saint Mary" showed that.

Like the old Negro spiritual says (paraphrasing), nobody knows the trouble I see, nobody knows my sorrow. Many times pain and suffering is an internal mental battle that can't be seen by others but the destructive damage is just as real.

However, the thing about pain, hardship, struggle, and suffering is it affects people in one or two ways. In most cases it builds character and turns one into a more caring human being or maybe even a saint. But, with a few it turns those into the most bitter and evil human being one can imagine.

Enough on this I must get back to my intended subject, in writing this article I never intended to get side tracked off into this entire Saint like stuff. It seems as if my pen just took over as character for a while and I had to snatch it back.

Now, about me revisiting my "No minimum wage" crusade. I truly believe that the survival of the USA and western civilization depends on completely getting rid of a minimum wage. If the minimum wage stays in place I don't believe it is possible for the USA or western civilization to survive, period.

No matter what the egg heads in Washington come up with it is impossible to save our welfare state. Their brains are scrambled, that is why they are called egg heads. Hell, anyone with a basic knowledge of economics should know that you can't get blood out of a turnip when none is there.

That same fact applies to food, money, or anything else, yet, these egg heads are making more and more people dependent on a well that is without a doubt about to dry up. It is sheer madness; even an idiot should understand that.

To continue doing something so shallow and stupid is a guarantee that there will be mass starving and social unrest that may take civilization all the way back to the stone age. Lord helps us.

The big enemy armored divisions of World War II ran on ball bearing and the strategy was to bomb the ball bearing factories out of existence. Well, the welfare state and big government power to control the free market place and private enterprise depends on having a minimum wage.

You can't have free enterprise or a free market place with government setting any labor price no matter how small or large. Sure, it was done in the name of helping the people like all social programs promised to do, but the Minimum wage gave a small baby welfare state a foot in the door and look at the beast we have today.

Any kind of government price or wage control over private production and distribution is a socialist or communist tactic and don't belong in our free enterprise capitalist system of government, period.

Of course, with no minimum wages people will earn less, but the things you buy would balance out and cost very little because business can never charge more than most people which are the poor can afford.

Getting rid of the minimum wage would stop all of this taxing everything that one can imagine, and then taxing would be limited to mostly real property of some sort.

After completely getting rid of the minimum wage, the next thing the government must do is protect the poor and disadvantage. And the only way to do that without destroying the free market place is for the government to establish government run commissaries, housing, and clinics and use tokens or script for all who qualify.

I promise you this USA and global economy is about to blow and the only way to bleed off the pressure is to eliminate the minimum wage, period. Otherwise, if they keep fiddling and allow a total collapse no one knows where it will end it may be all the way back to the Stone Age.

If the USA keep fiddling and don't get its duck all in a row this over the cliff thing will be just the tip of the Ice berg before total doom. I'm telling you not to ignore my warnings because I can dissect and understand an economy as well as anyone, just mark my words.

And another thing, these conservatives or anyone else out there that keep advocating big cuts in spending is out of their minds, it is too late for that.

They think they do but they don't truly understand economics. Sure, this economy is on the brink of a total collapse, but, with the mass amount of government dependents and debt load any drastic change in anything will instantly trigger the coming collapse right now, and no one wants that.

I, Freddie L. Sirmans, Sr. am suggesting the only course to save this great nation with freedom intact and prevent doomsday back to the Stone Age. The first thing that must be done is void and completely get rid of the minimum wage.

That will free up the people to save this great nation with freedom still intact, anything else is just buying a little more time. Getting rid of the minimum wage would allow the people themselves to save this great nation, which they can't do now because of the minimum wage and all kinds of government restrictions.

Big government and the welfare state can't save this great nation and have brought it to its knees and more taxes will just allow them to administer the coup de grace.

With no minimum wage to stop it the people can barter and hire each other as maid, handymen, or whatever to eat and survive, which they can't do now without wage and every other kind of government restriction. Soon millions will be starving sitting around waiting on government to save them.

Eliminating the minimum wage will allow the nuclear family to rebound and government can return to collecting taxes and protecting the country instead of snuffing out and lording it over the free market place.

Never forget the very poor and disadvantage still need a life line, and to keep from contaminating the free market place the government must establish government run commissaries, housing, and clinics and use tokens or script for those who qualify.

Sure, a change like this would be traumatic, but, freedom and the nation would survive, whereas, anything else is still doomsday bound or just plain wishful thinking.

I hear all of these people out here running their mouths, but, in my view they are just repeating what someone else said or don't have a clue as how to dissect an economy like I can. SIRMANS LOG: 8 DECEMBER 2012, 2008 HOURS

FLIMFLAM GAME IS WHAT DEMS ARE TRYING TO PULL OFF CONCERNING THIS "OVER THE CLIFF" THING.

The weakness with the republicans is they are putting the country first and want to do the right thing. Whereas that is the last thing on the minds of these dems and liberals, their first priority is to keep power by growing government and find a way to raise taxes and blame the resulting misery on the republicans.

I'm an independent, but that is why the republicans ought to tell them go fly a kite because we are never going to agree to raise taxes, period. But, doing that takes a lot of guts, and I for one am not sure the republicans have the guts to do that.

Besides, all of this "Lets make a deal" stuff is just a smoke screen by the Dems and liberals. Any one with an ounce of sense should know that the Dems and liberals are hard core tax and spenders, and never intend to cut spending or the growth of government under any condition no matter what they say.

There is no mystery about it growing government and doling out free goodies is what keeps them in power. Many times I have said that liberals were shallow and they are, but, I have never ever said that liberals were dumb.

Why do you think they have taken over and control almost every institution in this great free nation? Now, about this "Over the cliff" thing, the Dems and liberals have control of the reins, they really don't need the republicans for anything concerning this "Over the cliff" thing.

With one stroke of the pen the Dems and liberals leader can extend the Bush tax cuts at this very moment. But, there is a problem with doing that, doing that won't get them the tax increase and revenue they want to grow more government.

So, what they are really after is a way to kill two birds with one stone if they can make suckers out of the republicans. The way to do that is through negotiations, the two birds they are trying to kill is get their tax raise and blame it on the republicans at the same time.

They know the American public is dead set against a tax increase, except maybe on the falsely demonized rich.

They also know that they can't successful blame the republicans unless the republicans themselves agree to some type of tax increase.

So, maybe if they can just keep pounding away on taxing the demonized rich hopefully the republicans will cave and agree to some kind of tax increase on the rich or something of the sort, and if they do. Bingo, they got their prey, it doesn't matter, and any agreed tax increase by the republicans should serve their purpose.

Then with their liberal cohorts in the news media everything will be distorted, twisted, and blown way out of proportion. Now, the Bush tax cuts will be allowed to expire and guess who agreed to a tax increase and in their eyes is a valid blame?

Sure, they were going to end up blaming the republicans anyway but they see an agreed tax increase as the real thing. Now all you will hear is them mean old republicans who don't care about the poor or anyone, and is the reason for this big tax increase on the working people of America and on and on. It is the same old bait and switch liberal blame game strategy. SIRMANS LOG: 02 DECEMBER 2012, 1538 HOURS

WHERE IN THE "SAM HILL" IS THIS COTTON PICKING USA GOVERNMENT HEADED?

CAPITALISM: Is where private property ownership and individual freedom thrives. Almost all production and distribution is privately owned and operated for a profit.

It is a system where profit rules the day and just about everything else, no profit means nothing for the government to tax and survive on. Profit can only be generated with some type of business transaction. All salaries and everything else the government taxes can be traced back to the profit from some type of business transaction.

When you attack the rich and businesses you are attacking the very source that generates the profit that supplies the government with revenue (money).

Right now the American businesses can only generate 60 percent of the profit needed for our government to survive on, which means the government is borrowing the other 40 percent.

Yet, these insane Dems and liberals are hell bent on growing government even bigger with more debt, my God! This is sheer madness and twilight zone stuff that fails every sanity test. Maybe, it is
true that the Lord looks out for fools and crazy people, we as a nation are certainly going to need it.

As it stands most American businesses are barely surviving, some has a profit margin as small as 3 percent, and with a margin that low a few employees stealing a few items will put them out of business.

Yet, these shallow minded Dems and liberals are hell bent on putting several more layers of taxes on these hard working job providers, Lord, what a crying shame. For every business that the government tax forces out of business that means more unemployment and less tax money to the government.

I'm telling you these shallow minded Dems and liberals are stacking on layer by layer of even more taxes thereby breaking the backs of businesses. And, in effect destroying this last great land of individual freedom. We may end up back in the Stone age and that is no joke.

Plus, what is even worse 95 percent of the American population is too economically ignorant to even have a clue as to what is going on right before their eyes. That is especially true with the learned shallow surface dwelling predominate liberal news media.

SOCIALISM: Is where private ownership of property still exists but the government controls the production and distribution and what you can
do with your private property.

COMMUNISM: Is where there is no private property ownership and all production, distribution, and ownership is controlled by the government. And in my view it leads to everyone being equally poor except a privilege few, unless there is vast natural resources to sell on the open market.

If the Bush tax cuts are allowed to expire I believe it will drive so many businesses out of existance that the USA government will end up taking in far less tax revenue than it is taking in right now.

IN CLOSING: The only way to save the USA with our individual freedom still intact can be found throughout the writing of Freddie L. Sirmans, Sr. SIRMANS LOG: 30 NOVEMBER 2012, 1541 HOURS

DOOMS DAY MAY BE NEARER THAN WE THINK?

Here is my quick injection concerning this so-called physical over the cliff thing: This is sad for me to say, but, I don't think the Dems and liberals give a damn what financial disaster awaits the USA as long as
they can stay in power and find a way to blame it on the republicans.

When have a liberal ever accepted blame and took responsibility for anything unpleasant. Right now the liberals holds the reins for the safeguard and the direction this country will take into the future, but to listen to the bias liberal news media you would think the republicans is holding reins.

Here is what I think, I think the USA house leaders ought to tell the Dems, there won't be a tax increase on the American people on our part and then get the hell out of Dodge (meaning any negotiations). The fact is it is totally up to the Dems leader to let the Bush tax cuts expire or not.

So, go ahead, have your day, because no matter what happens the liberal media is going to blame the republicans for everything that turns out bad and nothing that turns out good anyway.

We had better thank God there is some resistance to these Tax and spend liberals, just look at Detroit and most of the northeast cities and the state of California to see what happens when liberals has no resistance and totally have their way. Sure, on this over the cliff thing the republicans are probably going to as usually cave big time.

Which, will just add one more layer of taxes on this nation and drive the dagger in a little deeper toward the heart and soul of this great nation? Like a broken record I will repeat, our welfare state cannot and will not survival, and I don't care what any learned anybody tells you, I'm telling you it is impossible for it to survive.

We will let history be the judge and I believe the wait is on horizon now. Mother Nature herself is not just free wheeling it, Mother Nature operates on set laws and the "Boom and bust" cycle is a law of nature.

The USA and world economy is long over due for a complete rebirth or renewal bust cycle by Mother Nature. There is no way man is going to stop it, the rotation is life itself, there is no life or existence for anything without a cycle.

The wisest thing man can do is prepare and get ready to try to survive and live past it, the bust cycle is on the horizon and the rotation must be completed for new growth and life to sprout anew. You will find the right answers and correct course to take throughout my writing, may the Gods be with you, Gods speed. SIRMANS LOG: 28 NOVEMBER 2012, 2104 HOURS

ANOTHER WORD OF WISDOM FROM THE GREAT THINKER (ME), FREDDIE L. SIRMANS, SR.

Most people are aware of the balance factor concerning government dependents on the dole becoming the majority voting population. Well, there is another balance factor that even the learned economist may not be keeping in mind.

This balance factor has to do with paying taxes. It stands to reason that no one is going to work if they are taxed at 100 percent. So, that means the government can tax up to a point with very little behavior change in the tax paying public.

But, once over a certain balance line there is going to be a drastic behavior change in the tax paying public. I'll bet anyone a dollar to a donut that we are on that line or even a little over it.

That means if the Dems succeed in getting a huge tax raise or allow the

Bush tax cuts to expire this USA government will end up taking in far less revenue than it is taking in now. Humans are complex beings that are motivated by a response to reward or punishment, which means no reward no motivation.

The liberals are too shallow to recognize the human factor; they see all people as just cogs in some giant machine. Our rich and well to do job providers are fed up. They are not stupid, why should they keep making great sacrifices to just be beaten down, spit upon, and robbed of their hard earned money by a spendthrift government.

They know a fair amount of taxes must be paid but their money was earned and belonged to them, whereas the liberal media and big government believes all earnings belong to the government and government is being generous to give you a little back.

You mark my word from here on out the more government taxes the less revenue it is going to take in. Now chew on that. In the authoritarian countries they stress the punishment side instead of the reward side to get people to produce and use fear with the promise if you don't work you don't eat.

But, in free countries like the USA and western Europe there is no longer hardly any fear factor left, many people get on the dole and will never do hard labor, especially hot farm labor.

So, I think in the coming months our dole and food stamp population is going to grow like a wild fire and drive the final nail in the coffin of this welfare state, or, at the very least cause a lot of pain and suffering. SIRMANS LOG: 18 NOVEMBER 2012, 1946 HOURS

THIS IS WHAT MUST BE DONE TO SAVE THIS GREAT NATION. ALSO, THIS IS THE RERUNNING OF THIS ARTICLE.

The reason why I don't think the polls will move very much in Mitt's favor is because we live in a welfare state which means we have masses upon masses of government's dependents that believe in big
government mind, body and soul.

And their one and only focus and interest is "What has government done for me lately." These dependents are bonded to the Democratic Party like a child is bonded to its mother.

That means these dependents will never be swayed with reason and logic, some where along the line an indelible stamp was put on their brain that the republicans is the enemy. And the only thing that can remove that stamp is to become an independent thinker.

However, no dependent thinker volunteers to become an independent thinker they must be forced to fend for themselves to become an independent thinker. All of that means these big government dependents are going to emotional support and vote democratic no matter how their candidate performs.

That is why I think it is short sighted to chase after people who will never vote republican under no condition, instead I think they should be pounding and pounding to no end lower taxes across the board, more jobs, and strong national defense with no regret, anything else only creates class envy.

It is very simple, if the republicans can't win with lower taxes "The inmates has already taken over the asylum" anyway. So, in the grand scheme of things, my final analysis is what do it really matter who win the election both candidates is determine to try to save save the welfare state.

In my view the welfare state is over done for and need to be buried, I think it is impossible for the USA and western civilization to survive unless the welfare state is abandon, period. Also, I think anyone that thinks the welfare state can be saved can't possible understand the free market or economics, period.

I may be wrong about a lot of things but without a doubt in my mind I know the welfare state can't possible be saved. With the damaged it has done to western civilization we will be lucky if we survive at all without going back to the Stone Age even if we abandon it today.

Otherwise Mother Nature is on the brink of stepping in herself, and I will tell you now if we don't act now a totally economic collapse is going to happy any day now. Unless my super natural wisdom advice is heeded western civilization is doomed in my view.

Yes, little old me has the answer. Again here is my survival solution, first get rid of the minimum wage entirely, rip it out by the root. Next, establish government run commissaries, housing, and clinics and use tokens or script for the poor, disadvantage, elderly, or whoever qualifies for aid.

Third void all taxes accept enough property tax for national defense, interior, and the operation of government, because it is going to come to that anyway when this economy soon totally collapse.

Forth, Government get the hell out of the free market, stay with collecting the taxes due, protecting and defending the country, and then the American people will save themselves and the government, too. But, to continue with this nanny state we have no chance of continuing to survive, period.

Hell, I know I'm not going to be taken serious, but, I'm a writer and I writer what I think, I can't make anyone believe or act upon anything I write, but, believe it or not at least it is food for though. And while I'm at it, another thing, everyone thinks the boom and bust cycle is a bad thing, wrong.

The boom and bust cycle is a law of

nature, and at some point the cycle must be completed. I believe time has finally ran out and the bust cycle is answering the call of nature and no matter what man does the bust cycle is going to complete its rotation.

I think nothing man does is going to stop it; I think all we can do is prepare to survive it. There are certain things throughout history that only Mother Nature's purges solved. Just look around at the USA, the anti-survival negative forces has just grown too powerful and only Mother Nature can bring them back under control.

Just look at the moral decay, the lack of family values, the murdering of the innocent unborn in the womb and on and on. When all of these negative anti-survival forces like men marring men and women marring women and all the rest becomes the norm a country is ripe to be taken over, there is no way in hell it can survive long term.

So, if man can't or won't deal with the

situation, nature's purges are sure to reset the clock. It has been proven in over 6,000 years of written history that the only way man can survive these purges of nature is with a strong nuclear and extended family system, a strong religious and moral code, and adequate emergency bartering capacity
with many small farmers and home gardeners.

Without these survival systems in place no civilization has ever been known to survive. Because of the "New deal" which birthed the welfare state, we have almost none of these survival systems left to survive nature's bust purge which is now coming upon us.

Our only hope is to act now before it fully hit, then it may be too late for the world. Lord, have mercy on the USA.
SIRMANS LOG: 4 OCTOBER 2012, 1327 HOURS

IT IS INSANE TO GIVE A

SPENDTHRIFT MORE REVENUE (MONEY) EXPECTING SOMETHING GOOD TO COME OF IT.

Giving a spendthrift more revenue (money) expecting a cure to the nation's financial problems is beyond dumb and stupid it is sheer madness.

The USA undoubtedly is living in fantasy land because in reality when you are 16 trillion in debt and still growing government you must be suicidal or have some kind of psychotic death wish. These liberals has gone stone mad.

I know as rule liberals are shallow with weak survival instincts, but, the American voters just recently gave them the reins and there is no way to snatch the reins from them. So, off the nations goes in full gallop into financial wonderland and shaking them won't work because this is not a dream.

I want to laugh but I can't because this is not a laughing matter we are all in this wagon as it heads toward the cliff.

I'm trying to snatch the reins in my writing but who the hell ever heard of Freddie L. Sirmans, Sr. and even if they did, my type of cure would be bitter medicine and this nation is not about taking any of it without going through a lot of hardship and suffering first.

When you see businesses and individuals making extreme profit and huge salaries that is because of big government and the welfare state. That is mainly due to lack of competition. You see, no matter what the shallow minded liberals may tell you, only local, state, and the federal government has the power to keep out the competition.

This is done with all kind of codes, licenses, fees, permits, regulations, etc. Sure, standards and qualification is needed but it don't end there the overkill is to keep out competition and the small guy.

Big government and big business scratches each others back, big business use government to price out competition and big government uses big business to push its social engineering agenda. However, big business can't force anybody to do anything whereas the government can.

Sure, big business has financial power and the money to pay huge teams of Philadelphia lawyers for awesome civil power, but that is about all.

My overall view is unless this government goes back to being a last resort for the poor and disadvantage where the nuclear family can rebound this great land of individual freedom will not survive as a free people, period.

As to the "Physical over the cliff" thing, my gut feeling is the republican house will end up caving, my God what a shame, but it is what it is. I could go on and on but I think you get my drift as to the state of the nation in my view.
SIRMANS LOG: 17 NOVEMBER 2012,

1420 HOURS

ANALYSIS OF THE 2012 PRESIDENTIAL ELECTION

First, here is a word of wisdom from the great thinker, you see, the general public as a whole has a herd mentality and really don't know what the hell they truly want.

The founding fathers were aware of this fact and that is the main reason we have a republic form of government. A republic is designed to select people that will lead not fall in line to follow an uninformed economic illiterate mob like herd with the use of insane polling.

There is no wonder why this nation may go over the cliff. Failing to realize this fact is the main reason the GOP keep loosing and unless things change we are going to lose this great free nation, too.

I, Freddie L. Sirmans, Sr. the great thinker and self-made writer have decided to give my opinion on the 2012 USA presidential election.

I see all of the pundits and so-called political experts on TV trying to get the tag number of that truck that just ran over them. Dick, Carl, and a few others still haven't figured out what hit them. Well, I for one would have been surprised if Mitt had won. But, I admit that I too had been swayed with this "The polls are wrong" nonsense.

Now, let's get down to the brass tacks of the matter; I think Romney ran an insane blank slate campaign. And anyone who reads my website knows I said that long before the election. Ronald Reagan would never have run a blank slate type of campaign like that.

Romney's main focus was to just attack the other guy which was a waste of time and money. These government dependents don't give a damn what their candidate has done or what he looks like as long as he is the candy-man and will keep the handouts and goodies coming.

Plus, everyone already knows who the Dems are; the Dems are the candy man, Santa Claus, and uncle shugga. And that means that is around 47 percent of the voters who is going to vote democrat no matter what come hell or high waters.

To these voters color of race has nothing to do with it they are bonded to the Dems like mother and child; they believe the republicans are going to kick their crutch from under them. And believe it or not I agree with them, I think it is cruel to kick a crutch from under anyone before first giving them some kind of emergency support system.

So, the republican candidate started off with 47 percent already in the Dems column. But, he still has 53 percent to win with. So, my advice to the GOP is to focus mainly on the 53 percent of voters you have the best chance to get.

The voters the GOP has the best chance of getting are small business owners, home owners, and anyone who believes in lower taxes. But, on that I'm probably spiting into the wind, because in my view one of the dumbest and stupidest things Romney and the GOP did was to all but abandon lower taxes.

They flat out let the Dems and liberals lay a guilt trip on them by making them feel guilty and ashamed to believe in and fight for lower taxes for all. Not me, I believe taxes are already too high for everyone in this country and taxes should be lowered across the board.

I'm not hearing this class warfare bull S**t, it is destroying this great country, and to me it is un-American and sick. If the Dems and liberals can't deal with it, tough titty, and to hell with them if they can't take a joke. Now, I have vented and cooled down.

All Romney had to do was pound and pound to no end lower taxes across the board, more jobs, and strong national defense. But, instead all he did was attack, attack, and head off in every direction and wallow in every controversial issue so no one really knew where he stood, and the votes he did get was "Anybody but Obama" in my view.

Believe me, I am not against Romney, what I'm writing may help someone else in the future. Romney now joins Dole and McCain as GOP presidential losers I believe because he too tried to out liberal a liberal for voters that will never vote republican under any circumstance.

There is no guarantee that what I advocate will produce a winner, but, at lease the people will know what the candidate fought for. No one knows what Dole, McCain, or Romney fought for except to be president. So, to all of these people on TV wondering about the GOP's future, just keep the faith.

The Dems are going to self-destruct, give them enough rope and they will. Just look at California and all of the big cities in the northeast, all are almost in ruins. Whoa, I almost forgot, in my view the GOP has a macho element to contend with, I think this element put a lot of pressure on Romney to go for blood and attack , attack even just for the sake of attacking.

The downside to that strategy in my view is it is a loser strategy, because you can't get your own message out and define who you are then even your own base can trust you. Well folks, I condensed it greatly but that concludes my analysis of the 2012 USA presidential election.
SIRMANS LOG: 11 NOVEMBER 2012, 1939 HOURS

REPUBLICANS MAY GET A SUPER MAJORITY IN BOTH HOUSES IN 2014!
Here is something the liberals and Dems need to be aware of because of the so called looming physical

economic over the cliff matter. This is something that can't be ignored and will determine if this great nation survives, period.

I think everyone knows that it is the Dems that is holding the reins. So, if the Dems botch this enough and cause enough pain and suffering all hell could break lose. After all the American voting public is a very fickle bunch and right or wrong has a herd instinct.

This physical cliff thing is no piece of cake and there is no easy way out left, the Dems are going to have to make some hard choices or face disaster.

A big enough screw up on this by the Dems could make the voters mad enough to award the GOP super majorities in both houses of congress in 2014. And that would make the president mostly a figure head after that. So, my answer to all of this is: Just the facts maam, just the facts.

I'm just saying, this is something the

Dems should just be aware of. Hell, I know the Dems are experts at blame shifting but in this case I doubt that blame shifting will be enough to placate the amount of pain and suffering going on.

Seeing the writing on the wall and not wanting to be entirely alone I look for this administration to bring on board a few Rockefeller type republicans.

I think they will look for big names like Colin Power, Richard Luger, etc. to put in high profile positions. That way at the very least the republican brand won't be entirely out of the picture. SIRMANS LOG: 8 NOVEMBER 2012, 1309 HOURS

THE DAY AFTER OBAMA'S WIN FOR FOUR MORE YEARS ANALYSIS
I, Freddie L. Sirmans, Sr. great self-made original thinking creative writer maybe should keep my views on this matter to my self, but, you know I'm going to vent anyway.

I totally disagree with this administration on almost everything. I believe the president believes totally the bigger the government the better, and the government is the answer to almost everything. I believe he thinks government should make sure everyone have an equal chance for a job and every benefit this country has to offer.

Now, on the surface all of the above sound fair and reasonable, but that is in theory. However, when actually put into practice there is a fatal flaw it that type of thinking, it doesn't work. It has never worked and never will for a simple reason, humans are not cogs in a machine.

Humans are complex emotional beings that are motivated by a response to reward or punishment, period. So, that being the case it means all of the president's policies now and in the future will never work in practice and are guaranteed to fail. But, never lose faith; there is a much bigger picture and message hidden here.

In my view the president is no ordinary man; I believe he is a man of destiny. I believe he truly wants to do what he feels is fair and best for all Americans all though I totally disagree with his method.

So, no Democrat would have dared open the door to China, but, republican Richard Milhouse Nixon did it. So, no republican will dare break the back of our welfare state, but, democrat Obama is going to do it if that is what it takes to save this great nation. "The Lord works in mysterious ways."

Disagree or dislike Obama if you must but this is a man who knows what it feels like to be different, looked down upon, or maybe even ridiculed. He has said many times "If one is willing to work hard everyone should have the opportunity to succeed in America. Remember the words, "Work hard."

So, I'm warning all of you government dependents out there falling over yourselves with Obama mania, you had better wake up; Obama can be the real Obama now. I'm sure Obama believes in socialism totally, but, I also believe this is a man that is not going to tolerate dead beat dads and people not working hard and pulling their share.

I believe the 'Lord works in mysterious ways." And this is a man guided by destiny and is here to break the back of the welfare state to save our nation whether he realizes it or not.

I, the great Destiny writer see a total economic collapse looming on the horizon. And for the sake of world balance, I don't believe Mother Nature will let this great land of individual freedom perish from the face of the earth forever.

Agree with me or not, that is my analysis of what is playing our on the world stage starring the USA as protagonist.
SIRMANS LOG: 07 NOVEMBER 2012, 1401 HOURS

OBAMA WINS FOUR MORE YEARS! THERE IS AN OLD SAYING, BE CAREFUL FOR WHAT YOU PRAY AND WISH FOR BECAUSE YOU JUST MIGHT GET IT. THAT SAID, THE AMERICAN PEOPLE HAS SPOKEN AND CHOSEN WHO WILL LEAD US FOR FOUR MORE YEARS.

THE LORD WORKS IN MYSTERIOUS WAYS. HOWEVER, I AM FOR INDIVIDUAL FREEDOM AND RESPONSIBILITY AND NOW BELIEVE THE WELFARE STATE INMATES HAS FINALLY TAKEN OVER.

WE AS A NATION ARE 16 TRILLION IN DEBT, WHAT'S UP WITH THAT. HOW MUCH OF OUR FREEDOM AND SOVEREIGNTY WILL BE SOLD OFF JUST TO TRY TO SAVE OUR UNSAVABLE WELFARE STATE? SIRMANS LOG: 6 NOVEMBER 2012, 2341 HOURS

LURKING ON THE HORIZON IS A

TOTAL WORLDWIDE ECONOMIC COLLAPSE!

As I, Freddie L. Sirmans, Sr. self-made great writer put pen to paper here on the eve of the big dance, meaning the 2012 USA presidential election. I'm just going to repeat what I have said before.

In the grand scheme of things it really doesn't matter a hill of beans who win this beauty contest. The reason why I believe this is because both candidates are hell bent on trying to save our welfare state, which I know is impossible. I don't care what the hell the learned economist or anyone else tells you, I'm telling you now it can't be done it is impossible, just keep living and you will see for yourself.

Now, here is the way it's going down, if the Dems win we can kiss individual freedom in the USA good by. And brace for the selling off of what's left of USA sovereignty. Also, I'm sure the Dems are going go all out for a complete power grab to gain absolute power for the welfare state.

As to the economy, the Dems will do nothing to prevent or prepare for the coming total world wide economic collapse, simply, because they are too shallow to even think something like that could possible happen until it is too late. Now, on the other hand if the GOP wins they will head off in another direction but still to no avail because the welfare state
can't be saved.

The GOP thinks they can put this welfare state beast on a diet to keep it from eating all of us alive, wrong. This welfare state beast has grown to strong and powerful for that and will end up making the GOP look like fools. In my view this beast is bloated with years of rot, moral decay, corruption, and inefficiency to the point that it will never allow any real rebirth and growth to save the USA.

This beast next step is going to be to bite off the hand that feed it. We all know that government survives on the taxes it collects. But, what few know and understand is that all tax money comes from private businesses and that is mostly small businesses. Even home owners and everyone else gets their income from a private business sources profit.

It is simple; survival of government depends on private profit, profit, and more profit, with one exception slavery or something like slavery. Nothing the government does produce a profit, only a private business transaction can generate a profit. Government can simply kill all businesses just by taking to much of their profit where they won't be able to restock and pay others expenses.

Being rich is an attitude and around ninety percent of the people don't have that attitude. Rich people are not the same as poor people with money, they have a whole different mindset. There never has and never will be a wealthy nation without a lot of rich people to make it happen. Rich people are the life blood of every free nation that is why a dictator or anyone against individual freedom will go after and try to destroy the rich.

There is a reason why almost all of the world is poor and will always be poor; it is the crab syndrome, because those in power will not allow a true free market place. A government that allows a free market place with free competition and doesn't siphon off all of the profit will never remain poor, but, those in power almost never allow that.

People are not stupid, no one is going to work hard and produce a lot of profit if government is just going to take almost all of it away. That is why socialism and communism always make everyone equally poor except a privilege few.

I can dissect an economy as well as anyone, now, you are going to tell me I don't know what the hell I am talking about when I say the welfare can't be saved, what a joke, get real.
SIRMANS LOG: 06 NOVEMBER 2012,

0051 HOURS

ROUND #3 AND THE FINAL 2012 PRESIDENTIAL ELECTION DEBATE, A QUICK BRIEF ANALYSIS BY ME, FREDDIE L. SIRMANS, SR.

What the hell does it really matter, it is all scripted anyway. Nothing is real anymore as to what the candidate really stands for, it is all fake and window dressing driven by what showed up on a poll, its fiction and rehearsed, and whoever is the most flamboyant with the best gift of gab usually wins.

That is why the sages of old and the founding fathers almost to a man never trusted a democracy and is the reason we actually have a republic.

So, like I have said many times before, in the grand theme of things the welfare state can't be saved and both candidates is hell bent on trying to do just that, it is insane, trying to save the un-savable, what a joke, and sad situation in my view.

But, who cares what the hell I think! I'm seen as a nut case out here whistling Dixie, next patient please. SIRMANS LOG: 23 OCTOBER 2012, 0412 HOURS

UNDERSTANDING NATURE'S BOOM AND BUST CYCLES!

The boom and bust economic cycles in life is just like the life and death cycles, it is a necessity for long term survival. There is no escape from them because they are part of natures design.

Everyone seems to think that an economy only involves money, wrong, trade and bartering is the foundation of every economy and has existed long before a currency was invented.

Sure, a currency is an evolutionary advancement in trade and bartering, but, never forgets, you can't eat material possessions, and it may come a time when a garden and a shotgun is worth more than two or three million dollars.

Man can stave off the bust cycle, but only so long and at a price, and that price is the longer the delay the greater the destruction when the bust cycle rotation finally purges the old to allow a new sprout to begin.

And in our case it may take civilization all the way back to the stone age, but, none of that has to happen if the USA first get rid of the minimum wage completely and follow other steps laid out in my writing.

Right now we have almost no emergency survival backup tools left in terms of raw bare boned survival. All throughout history a strong nuclear and extended family system, a strong religious and moral code, and adequate emergency backup bartering capacity with many small farmers and home gardeners would keep us fed through any bust cycle, like the great depression. But, now almost all of those tools has been destroyed by the welfare state.

In terms of sheer survival we as a nation have almost no chance of surviving a total economic collapse, we the USA and the civilize world may very well go back to the stone age, that is why I cry and preach so hard of the wisdom of ripping out this minimum wage demon to save our nation.

The ripping out and complete elimination of the minimum wage is a start back to basics and the only thing that is going to give this nation a fighting chance and even that may be too late. I can't stress the wisdom of eliminating the minimum wage enough no matter how sick and tired people get of hearing it.

Just like death is not the end all, but only one half of nature's life and death cycle the same applies to natures economic bust cycle. The economic bust cycle looms on the horizon, what are we the great USA going to do to survive it.

For over 6000 years man has had the

same above said tools in place to survive any economic bust cycle. But, now starting with the "New deal" that created our welfare state beast those tools are very weak to nonexistence. Time a wasting, what are we the USA going to do, get rid of the minimum wage or not, we must prepare to stand alone if we must because it's going to be every nation for itself soon.

Maybe, we are going to just keep fiddling and graciously accept going back to the Stone Age. I pray we will not, but I have no power except my pen, and no one has to believe a word I say, let along act on anything I say. SIRMANS LOG: 16 OCTOBER 2012, 1407 HOURS

FREDDIE L. SIRMANS, SR. OPENS UP HIS SOUL TO HIS READERS FOR ALL TO SEE WHAT MAKES HIM TICK

Folks I don't do this often and this is the first time I have shared this much of my inner self. In this brief article I

am going to talk only about me.
Sometimes I wonder what the hell
happened to me; I never set out
to be in any kind of political arena.

Why, why oh Lord, this is the last thing
that I ever wanted is to be in any kind
of public limelight. But, here I am as a
great raw crude self-made creative
writer commenting on the political
stage and being driven by some
unknown force to make my economic
and political views
known.

You see, all throughout my childhood I
suffered an inferior complex, but some
where deep down in my soul there was
a fighting instinct to survive at all cost.
No matter how many times I was told
that I would never amount to anything
I knew different.

I never have and never will feel
completely comfortable and normal in
a public setting. But, I'm still human
and cry, bleed, and feel pain the same
as other human beings. Also, I believe
that I have been blessed with

119

exceptional wisdom, talent, and ability that very few appreciate or understand.

I have no monopoly on past hardship or suffering but I think I have certainly had my share. No one can acquire the deep wisdom that I have without enduring a lot of struggle in life. I don't attend church as much as I should but I am spiritual to the core.

I learned very young that those that can genuine love and forgive can never be mentally defeated. I believe genuine talent and ability is like a liquid in that it will always eventually seek it own level if one stay the course and never quit. I know the average reader will never understand my writing and most can't take it after a few paragraphs.

There is no reason for me to fret because if my ability and talent have what it take all of the kings horses and all the kings' men can't stop it from seeking its own proper level, and I will get my due. There, I have opened up my soul so my readers can judge the human side of me.

Sorry, if some see this as just plain self serving, but sometimes it is OK as far as I'm concern to just bare ones soul. This is insight into who I am and what I think.
SIRMANS LOG: 12 OCTOBER 2012, 1709 HOURS

A TOTAL ECONOMIC COLLAPSE LOOMS ON THE HORIZON, AND WHAT DO THE USA DO, FIDDLE WHILE ROME BURNS.

When they win I'm sure the GOP plan on doing the normal good intention thing by balancing the budget, but, that can't be done in an out of control welfare state without growing the dole roll. Saving the welfare state is an impossible task.

Sure, your intentions are good, but, remember, "The road to hell is paved with good intentions." Doing the most sensible thing is what really counts, and it sure ain't trying to save an unsolvable burned out system.

I believe a total economic collapse is inevitable and is going to happen soon, no one knows when, hell, I have been pounding this same warning now for nearly twenty years. Still, no one listens or take my wisdom and warnings seriously.

Since we all know it is going to happen and man can't stop it, I think the wisest course is to prepare to withstand and survive an all out total economic collapse. Now, concerning the upcoming presidential election, I believe the GOP would preserve our freedom and buy more time for a miracle to come along and save us from a total economic collapse.

But, now I'm not so sure anymore. Under normal circumstance the GOP would definitely buy us more time, but the problem is we have a hungry welfare state beast on our hands and there is not enough money in the entire world to keep it fed.

Both presidential candidates are hell bent on saving the welfare state at all cost and there lies the problem in my view. I think trying to save the welfare state is an impossible task and economic suicide. We all know with the Dems it is a lost cause they are going to continue to tax and spend this nation and our freedom out of existence, that is a given.

But, you see, the GOP is also hell bent on feeding this same beast, but, trying to put it on a lesser spending diet. The GOP I believe intends to cut, manage, and try to make sense of a burned out unworkable and
doomed system. Which, I'm sure in actuality will speed up the demise of the whole system.

Directly or indirectly the profit from private business and mostly small businesses is the sole support that keeps government operating. And for a long time now that support has not been able to keep our welfare state beast fed. So, higher taxes will mean even less profit from small business for government to tax.

Now, if the GOP starts cutting and slashing we will end up with a smaller pie that must feed the same amount of needy greedy dependent mouths. No one believes in independency and self-sufficiency more than I do, but, I think it is cruel to kick a crutch from under anyone unless they have some type of lifeline to hold on to.

Like a broken record here I go again on what I think must be done for this nation to survive. First, rip the minimum wage up by the root and eliminate it entirely, then burn it where it can't come back. Next, to give the poor, the disadvantage, and elderly a lifeline, the government should establish government run commissaries, housing, and clinics.

Also, the government should issue tokens or script to all who qualify for these services to keep from causing inflation in the free market national currency. Next, the government must never give anyone free unearned money but still pay hard currency to those that work for the government.

Doing it this way will stop contaminating the national free market currency and will stop driving the cost of living out of sight for everyone. And lastly, government ought to void all taxes except on physical property and then only enough for national defense, interior, and the operation of government.

Hell, I know this is extreme but do we really have a choice? Because A total collapse is coming anyway and the most we can do is try to survive and live through it, mother natures bust cycle will not be denied. But, at least this way if we act first we should be able to survive with our freedom still in tact.

I know my advice will be ignored but at least it will give wise men something to think about, "A word to the wise is sufficiency."

SIRMANS LOG: 7 OCTOBER 2012, 1252 HOURS

HOW TO SAVE USA AND GLOBAL ECONOMY: "GOOD GOVERNMENT IS A PROTECTOR NOT A PROVIDER!"

MY ANALYSIS ON ROUND 1 OF THE 2012 PRESIDENTIAL DEBATE SERIES.
Let me, Freddie L. Sirmans, Sr. the great self-made writer weigh in. It was not even close in my opinion, Mitt won by a country mile. But, I doubt the polls will move very much in his favor.

Folks, I'm a writer and I'm not running for anything now or ever, so that leaves me free to shoot from the hip and many times I'm wrong, but even a stopped clock is right twice a day.

The reason why I don't think the polls will move very much in Mitt's favor is because we live in a welfare state which means we have masses upon masses of government's dependents

that believe in big
government heart, body and soul.

And their one and only focus and
interest are "What has government
done for me lately." These dependents
are bonded to the Democratic
Party like a child is bonded to its
mother.

That means these dependents will
never be swayed with reason and
logic, some where along the line an
indelible stamp was put on their
brain that the republicans is the
enemy. And the only thing that can
remove that stamp is to become an
independent thinker.

However, no dependent thinker
volunteers to become an independent
thinker they must be forced to fend for
themselves to become an independent
thinker. All of that means these big
government dependents are going to
emotional support and vote democratic
no matter how their candidate
performs.

That is why I think it is short sighted to chase after people who will never vote republican under no condition, instead I think they should be pounding and pounding to no end lower taxes across the board, more jobs, and strong national defense with no regret, anything else create class envy.

It is very simple, if the republicans can't win with lower taxes "The inmates has already taken over the asylum" anyway. So, in the grand scheme of things, my final analysis is what do it really matter who win the election anyway both candidates is determine to save the welfare state.

In my view the welfare state is over done for and need to be buried, I think it is impossible for the USA and western civilization to survive unless the welfare state is abandon, period. Also, I think anyone that thinks the welfare state can be saved can't possible understand the free market or economics, period.

I may be wrong about a lot of things
but without a doubt in my mind I
know the welfare state can't possible
be saved. With the damaged it
has done to western civilization we will
be lucky if we survive at all
without going back to the Stone Age
even if we abandon it today.

Otherwise mother nature is on the
brink of stepping in herself, and I
will tell you now if we don't act now a
totally economic collapse is going
to happy any day now. Unless my
super natural wisdom advice is
heeded western civilization is doomed
anyway in my view.

Yes, little old me has the answer.
Again here is my survival solution, first
get rid of the minimum wage entirely,
rip it out by the root. Next, establish
government run commissaries,
housing, and clinics and use tokens or
script for the poor, disadvantage,
elderly, or whoever qualifies for aid.

Third void all taxes except enough
property tax for national defense,

interior, and the operation of government, because it is going to come to that anyway when this economy soon totally collapse.

Forth, Government get the hell out of the free market, stay with collecting the taxes due, protecting and defending the country, and then the American people will save themselves and the government, too. But, to continue with this nanny state we have no chance of continuing to survive, period.

Hell, I know I'm not going to be taken serious, but, I'm a writer and I writer what I think, I can't make anyone believe or act upon anything I write, but, believe it or not at least it is food for though. And while I'm at it, another thing, everyone thinks the boom and bust cycle is a bad thing, wrong.

The boom and bust cycle is a law of nature, and at some point the cycle must be completed. I believe time has finally ran out and the bust cycle

is answering the call of nature and no
matter what man does the bust
cycle is going to complete its rotation.

I think nothing man does is going to
stop it; I think all we can do is
prepare to survive it. There are certain
things throughout history that
only Mother Nature's purges solved.
Just look around at the USA, the
anti-survival negative forces has just
grown too powerful and only
Mother Nature can bring them back
under control.

Just look at the moral decay, the lack
of family values, the murdering of
the innocent unborn in the womb and
on and on. When all of these
negative anti-survival forces like men
marring men and women marring
women and all the rest becomes the
norm a country is ripe to be taken
over, there is no way in hell it can
survive long term.

So, if man can't or won't deal with the
situation, natures purges are
sure to reset the clock. It has been

proven in over 6,000 years of written history that the only way man can survive these purges of nature is with a strong nuclear and extended family system, a strong religious and moral code, and adequate emergency bartering capacity with many small farmers and home gardeners.

Without these survival systems in place no civilization has ever been known to survive. Because of the "New deal" which birthed the welfare state, we have almost none of these survival systems left to survive nature's bust purge which is now coming upon us.

Our only hope is to act now before it fully hit, then it may be too late for the world. Lord, have mercy on the USA.
SIRMANS LOG: 4 OCTOBER 2012, 1327 HOURS

I CAN'T POUND IT ENOUGH, THE MINIMUM WAGE MUST GO!
OK, lately I have kept up this constant

drum beat to eliminate the minimum wage. There is a deep reason for that, that doesn't meet the eye of those with little depth and perspective. To me the minimum wage roots grow far deeper than wages and what one earns.

To me the minimum wage is the foundation and corner stone of the welfare state. If the minimum wage was eliminated nation wide it would be the first step back to a true free market place economy. And if that was followed up by separating government spending from the national economy a miracle would take place.

The problem with the USA economy is it is being used like in an incest relationship and is feeding on it's self. You See the government itself is what driving up consumer inflation out of sight. The government is taking tax payers money and giving it free unearned to the poor and thereby driving up the cost of living on the tax payers and everyone.

Food stamps and unearned money given to some citizens by the government flood what little left of a free market we have and contaminates it by providing a big enough pool of payers to prevent any reduction in prices.

Sure, I feel as a last resort the government must help the poor and disadvantage. But, the only way the government can help the poor and others without destroying the free market place is by establishing government run commissaries, housing, and clinics and using tokens or script for those that qualify.

Doing it this way will keep government spending separated and out the free market and prevent contamination by not driving up the cost of living on the tax payers. It is simple you can't have a true free market economy with a minimum wage.

There is this false assumption that booms and busts cycles are a bad thing. Sure, no one likes to loose money or go out of business, but cycles are a must for survival, period. It is a law of nature that everything must have a cycle to exist; there must be life and death to maintain life.

Life could not be maintain with life only or death only, with life only one thing would crowd out the universe. Man does have the ability to manipulate and extend the economic cycle for longer periods of time, but according to the law of nature the cycle must be completed sooner or later.

However, to extend the life of an economy too long comes with a big price, that price is it allows the anti-survival and negative forces in life to become more and more powerful. There is no such a thing as something all good or all bad. Everything is relative in some way; too much of a good thing is bad.

So, in an economy when you don't allow small purges like business failures which is the bust cycle to get rid of and prevent the build up of rot, moral decay, and inefficiency you become an enabler to the growth of anti-survival forces. And the longer man puts off the bust cycles by bailing out and propping up rot, decay, and inefficiency the more drastic action must be taken.

If nature's supreme law of natural selection have to step in then it may mean back to the Stone Age. Right now it is too late, the USA government will never save the economy from a total collapse, but I will tell you what will, take my advice in this article.

Start by first eliminating the minimum wage, next separate government spending from the free market national economy. To sum it up, eliminate the minimum wage and get as close as possible to a true free marker place, then the USA will survive with freedom intact.

Otherwise, the whole world may go back to the stone age. I am saying again, and again, and again, the minimum wage must go, not lowered, but ripped out by the root, or else. SIRMANS LOG: 26 SEPTEMBER 2012, 2351 HOURS

GOP AND DEMS HORSE RACE IN DEAD HEAT ROUNDING CURVE INTO FINAL STRETCH!

Ok, Ok, now they are approaching the final turn going into the home stretch to win the big November 2012 USA presidential election sweep stake. Folks, look like its going to be a photo finish by a nose.

I, Freddie L. Sirmans, Sr. self-made great writer will give a quick analysis on winning or losing a race like this. And at this stage it is still too close to call, no one truly knows who the winner will be. To be fair I must say up front that I am bias because of my conservative and in many cases extreme views, I'm for small government and low taxes.

Now, let me delve into the meat of the subject, I think the only different between the two horses is how fast we loses our freedom after the election. That is because to maintain civil order we as a country must eliminate the "Minimum wage" or turn into a dictatorship or some other form of authoritarian rule.

I believe within the next four years they are going to finish selling off the rest of USA sovereignty to support the welfare state. And that is going to cause mass uprisings that will lead to martial law and finally dictatorship or authoritarian rule. Wow! I'm getting too far off track, let me get back to the 2012 horse race.

I believe if the Dems win we will lose our freedom at a quick rapid fire pace, whereas if the GOP win we will lose it at a drip by drip pace, but, at least the latter will allow more time for a possible miracle to save our freedom.

My take is the GOP has decided to run their horse with a blank slate strategy and use an attack and drive

up the other horse's dislike-ability.
I think it is an insane strategy, but,
who knows it may really work. I
think they figure the liberal media
won't have a big target to shoot at
and they can drive up the Dems
horse's dislike-ability enough to pull of
at least a narrow victory.

Who knows they may be right.
However, overall I beg the difference;
I
think that strategy is just too risky.
Sure, a lot of voter may vote for you
because they hates the other horse
more, but in most cases that is just
not going to be enough.

So, the main flaw I see in that strategy
is it is just too risky in my view, plus, I
see another reason why that is unlikely
to work. In my view when dealing with
Dems and liberals you are not dealing
with reasonable and rational beings in
terms of long term USA survival. They
want their government goodies now, to
hell with y'all and long term survival of
the whole nation.

Sure, they are good and decent Americans and I love them dearly. But, after years and years of socialist/liberal media indoctrination true reality has yet to set in. There are millions upon millions that believe government help will always be there to aid them not realizing that there has never been and never will be a government that didn't go broke at some point.

And I give this government four years at most, but, of course I pray that I'm wrong. Back to the horse race, Even if the GOP did succeed in their strategy, which they won't because the liberal media will never allow it.

But, even if they did brand the Dems horse as a terrible socialist, all would happen is the masses of government dependents would say he is our socialist and we know he will protect and take care of us, and prove it with their vote. That is the facts and why I think the bland strategy is severely flawed.

I am only writing my views and

opinions, no one really knows, the bland strategy could still hit pay dirt. My low taxes, more jobs, and strong national defense advocacy is risky too, especially in today's liberal hollering high tax climate. I'm one that believe in "No guts no glory," Take a stand you believe in and fight tooth and nails to defend it, some one has to lose.

The three things I have strongly advocated has long been proven guaranteed GOP winners, which is lower taxes, more jobs, and strong national defense. But, in my view the GOP no longer believe in them or doesn't have the gut to run on them, especially lower taxes, how sad.

Hell, if the GOP can't still win on lower taxes and more jobs, "The inmates has already taken over the asylum, anyway," but I don't believe that has actually happened, yet. Even if one loses, stand for your beliefs, freedom means standing for what you believe in.

Washington standing tall in the boat crossing the Delaware, everyone without a doubt knew what he was standing for. Agree or not that is my analysis of the November 2012 big presidential horse race fixing to go into the final stretch.

Like I've said before I am just a lone neurotic self-made writer with super natural God give wisdom, what the hell do I know? So far no one ever seems to pay any attention to a damn thing I say, still, I enjoy writing and expressing my views. I dearly love this great country, the only one I know.
SIRMANS LOG: 24 SEPTEMBER 2012, 1414 HOURS

THE MINIMUM WAGE IS STANDING IN THE WAY OF USA SURVIVAL!
Right now the USA has more ability to survive on it's own than any nation on earth. In raw talent, ability, and natural resources the USA is unsurpassed.

The problem with the USA is it has allowed the liberals and their welfare state to get a deadly choke hold on the nation neck and we are being strangled to death. The ultra high taxes and murdering regulations are slowly killing this great nation. It is too late now the USA government no longer has the wisdom or the will to save this great nation in my view.

The ever increasing high taxes and choking regulations will in a couple of years make it impossible for private business to make enough profit to survive. And the economically ignorant general public doesn't have a clue that all government funding originates from the profit of private business.

So, very soon our welfare state ain't gonna have the funds to save anyone, it is already flat broke and you can juggle the books and run schemes but only so long. As of now the people themselves are the only thing that can save the great USA.

They can still save the great USA by buying, selling, and maybe even bartering with each other to feed themselves and survive, after all people traded and bartered for thousands of years before money was invented.

In fact the American Indian survived for centuries and never had a currency. To survive sometimes you gotta do what you gotta do. One must have food, shelter, and warmth to survive, then every thing else is gravy when times get hard enough.

Going this route hopefully the government can still tax enough to maintain security if nothing else, at this stage this is the wisest course to take. Otherwise if we keep trying to save the welfare state I guarantee you we will end up with a dictator or some form of authoritarian rule, and if that happens 100 million starving to death will be a low figure in my view.

There is no doubt in my mind if allowed to the people will take the bull by the horns and do whatever it take to survive. The people can and will save the great USA but there is a problem, as it is they can't, even it being the last chance and hope for USA survival.

You see, the "Minimum wage is standing right dab in the middle of the way and if it is not ripped up by the root and completely eliminated it is over for the great USA, we will be totally doomed. I have pounded and pounded this fact to no end all to no avail everyone seems to think I'm crazy.

But, where there is a will there is always a way and I still have hope. So, as long as there is still breath in my body I will be pounding for the elimination of the minimum wage. Just maybe enough people will wake up before it is too late.

Thank you God for my life, health, and strength, I am truly blessed and have so much to live for, thank you, thank you, thank you...

SIRMANS LOG: 14 SEPTEMBER 2012,
1905 HOURS

WELL, I GUESS I FINALLY LOST MY COTTON PICKING MIND

I am only one man, a pitiful looking little neurotic handicap armed only with a pen going up against this awesome almighty omnipotent welfare state. It is just like the classic battle of David going up against Goliath armed only with a slingshot.

I think in about four years the socialist/liberal news media is going to be the most surprised of all. That is because they are the first ones that must go when a dictator or an authoritarian government starts consolidating power.

Like I've said before I believe the economy is going to totally collapse within four years. That being the case I think the take over will start with martial law, and then a dictator or some type of authoritarian regime will emerge.

The only thing that is going to save the America economy from a totally collapse is the complete elimination of the minimum wage, period, nothing else can save us. Mainly because the welfare state have destroyed any backup or safely valve to survive on like a strong nuclear and extended family system.

The things that allowed civilization to survive for over 5,000 years like a strong nuclear and extended family system, strong moral and family values, and adequate emergency backup bartering capacity with many, many small farmers and home gardeners are all almost nonexistent.

We have almost no means of surviving when the economy totally collapses. And that is a fact that the liberals are too shallow to ever see until people starts starving by the millions. It is completely get rid of the minimum wage or back to the Stone Age, there is no other option.

I'm no fool I know today's politicians will never totally eliminate the minimum wage, still, I must never stop pounding and pounding away because it is my destiny and duty to keep sounding the distress call, come hell or high waters. God save America.
SIRMANS LOG: 12 SEPTEMBER 2012, 2049 HOURS

AGAIN, THE MINIMUM wage MUST BE RIPPED UP BY THE ROOT AND COMPLETELY ELIMINATED.
I know a lot of people don't understand my thinking and writing, but, I'm not just out here free wheeling it there is a method to my insanity or wisdom that guides me.

So, let me shine some light on what guides me. The reason I know without a shadow of a doubt that I am right and in time will be vindicated is because my thinking is in line with nature's supreme law of "Natural selection."

A society must have government for the protection of the whole society, but, pertaining to the economy government involvement and force is the worst thing you can have. That is because force flies into the face of nature's supreme law of "Natural selection."

The law of "Natural selection" is what controls everything and all existence, and it is based on a survival need. If there is no survival need for it, any and everything starts ceasing to exist. The old saying is really true, "If you don't use it you lose it."

So, when government forces a "Minimum wage" on the people the ability to hire people at any cost starts ceasing to exist. Even a giant mighty oak tree didn't start big but instead started from a wee little acorn.

The "Minimum wage" must be ripped up by the root and completely eliminated if the USA and western civilization is to have any chance of survival. Otherwise, according to nature's supreme law of "Natural selection" it will be impossible for the USA to survive as 57 states, every special interest group and faction in the nation will soon be at each others throat.

There will be no way of avoiding it, back to the Stone Age will be our destination. I know that around 99.9 percent of the American people think I'm insane for wanting to completely get rid of the minimum wage, still that don't prove me wrong.

God has blessed me with this great super natural wisdom for a reason. No matter how handicapped or seemingly unqualified I may be the distress call must be sounded and go forth regardless, it is my destiny and it is bigger than my well being or survival.

This whole thing is like the classic battle of good versus evil. There are some who think my way of thinking represents evil by wanting to set things back to when many didn't have certain rights. But, I'm not about taking away anyone's rights I am strictly against anything of the sort.

What I am about is saving human beings and many of the old values is what allowed civilization to survive for over 5,000 years. The nuclear family, good moral values, and adequate bartering capacity are a must, and without them no society can survive for very long, period.

Today in the USA every one of those three values is in almost total ruins. I have no bitterness towards anyone; I know I can see much more than the average person in term of survival.

An example is like many people that have been severely injured or had something bad happen to them, but later said they was glad it happened because it opened their eyes, and they can now see things that was always right before their eyes.
SIRMANS LOG: 8 SEPTEMBER 2012,

1026 HOURS

CAN GENERAL MOTORS WITHSTAND THE TEST OF TIME?

Folks, I try to leave certain things alone, but I just couldn't hold my tongue any longer or I was going to pop if I didn't vent. What I am talking about is all of this bragging by the shallow minded liberals about saving general motors.

Well, I for one have a different opinion about that matter. In my view liberals just simply doesn't have the depth to understand democracy or the free market, period. Our liberal created welfare state is what has created all these shallow minded liberals that are coming out of the woodworks armed with unsound judgment.

The liberals have not saved general motors what they really have done is made it another big government dependent. The very basics of understanding life, growth, and survival, or just existence itself are to know that you have to get rid of rot, decay, and inefficiency.

You just simply can't have progress, growth, and long term success without allowing failure. What government has actually done to general motors is create another burden on the American tax payers. And from now on it will always be a burden because its management will never make the hard decisions to get rid of enough rot, decay, and inefficiency to become totally independent and profitable.

Sure, it is propped up now, but this government is broke and will soon be going under, then what? This nation has bankruptcy laws which mean general motors would have survived, but leaner and meaner, I think saving the unions and keeping liberal voters happy definitely was a factor. But, instead we have a wobbly kneed colossal big government dependent for life.

In closing, I'm just one self-made neurotic writer with an opinion, what the hell do I know?
SIRMANS LOG: 6 SEPTEMBER 2012, 2337 HOURS

WHAT DO AFRICANS AMERICANS AND WOMEN HAVE IN COMMON?

What do African Americans and women have in common; they both have a very high dependency mentality. This is not intended to put these two demographics down in any way; this is to try to understand the why of this phenomenon.

Plus, I don't think this is necessarily a bad thing, it allowed African Americans as a race to survive in a hostile environment right out of slavery. But, this is a new day and it is time for African Americans as a race to think as individuals and be more responsible for their own survival.

When are Africans Americans on a wide scale going to provide more of their own businesses to provide jobs and do more of the hiring of their own people, cry me a river? I am retired now, but over the years I have hired people and provided jobs.

On a mass scale what the hell survival need can a poor black man offer a woman when uncle sugar is her Great white father provider, you tell me. To act responsible there must be a survival need to be responsible according to nature's supreme law of "Natural selection."

The welfare state has just about taken all responsibility away from the poor black man in the African American community, and the rest of the nation will soon follow suit. So, how can you expect someone to be responsible when they have never been conditioned to be responsible, you can't logically? I totally blame the shallow minded liberals for this situation.

As a writer I am only trying to get at the facts and wade through all of the myths and emotionalism. I'm one that believes that almost nothing about life is innate; it is all learned in some way. I believe a new born baby's brain starts off as a clean slate.

So, there must be a logical reason why 90 percent plus African Americans as a group always vote for one political party. It is like the unbreakable bond between a mother and child. In my books and writings I go deep into the reasons why African Americans think the way they do.

But, for now I will move on to the political reality of dealing with the said two demographics groups. If conservatives and republicans are thinking about winning these two groups over with reason, forget it, it ain't gonna happen. There is an emotional bond here with the Democratic Party that can't be broken with no amount of reasoning.

These two groups see the Democratic Party like a child sees its parents. It is all about dependency versus independency. Dependency is the nesting syndrome, and the only way to break the nesting syndrome is to kick the dependent out of the nest, that is what the mother eagle does.

But, for African Americans, mentally we are still in the nest and will stay there as long as we have a welfare state. And the really sad part is the welfare state has almost totally destroyed the African American culture and nuclear family and is fast working on the entire nation.

And another thing, the poverty pimps are making sure that African Americans never leave the safety of the nest. They guarantee that African Americans won't ever be able to jettison their dependency slave mentality.

African Americans still mentally see the master's beer as colder and if given a choice won't automatically support his look alike brothers and sisters in business or otherwise.

The African American elite won't create zones in and around an all African American neighborhood to live but instead get as far away as they can afford.

Sure, the excuse now is crime is the big problem but I don't buy that for one second as the only reason, because the movie "A raising in the sun" showed escaping from black neighborhoods long before the welfare state kicked the black man out of the home to create all of this crime.

I see a culture problem here, but the poverty pimps are still fighting both tooth and nails to keep African Americans in the nest as helpless victims, instead of taking more responsibility for our own survival come hell of high waters.

As a race we owned and controlled far more before the welfare state came along and destroyed the black community. My God what a sad situation, still, I wish all people

goodwill including the good intention
poverty pimps.

It is the welfare state that has created
all of these dependents and if
they haven't reached a majority yet it
is only a matter of time before
they do and send us all back to the
Stone Age.

I think we still have a majority in hard
working tax payers and
independents that will give
conservatives and republicans a
political Trifecta in November but just
barely, on one condition.

That one condition is the republicans
must pound and pound to no end
low taxes, more jobs, and strong
national defense. Otherwise, Lord
knows I hope I'm wrong, but I just
don't believe the republicans can
win it otherwise.

Myself, I am a conservative at heart
but in practice I'm a realist.
SIRMANS LOG: 31 AUGUST 2012,
1303 HOURS

CURRENT EVENTS: WHY CRUCIFY ONE FOR A BAD CHOICE OF WORDS?

This abortion flap going around that is supposed to be so outrageous is only a modern thing. Until within the last one hundred years an unborn child conceived through rape was almost never killed.

In fact some believe that the child itself acts as a healing process from a horrible traumatic event. Back then the racial element was the only thing that guaranteed the killing of the unborn child of the rape victim in some cases.

So, in my opinion why should a poor choice of words create all of this ado about something the moral bankrupted liberals would like to exploit? And all liberals are not democrats. This is the sort of thing that can end up biting the self-righteous.

What is freedom if a man can't defend

the unborn, we have no future if
no one defends the unborn. It's no
wonder social security is going
under we have killed off a whole
generation of payers.
SIRMANS LOG: 21 AUGUST 2012,
0150 HOURS

FAR TOO MANY AMERICANS ARE JUST PLAIN ECONOMICALLY IGNORANT!

Economically speaking "What belongs
to everyone belongs to no one," in
theory, maybe not, but, in actually
practice it's definitely true.

Okay, this idea that the government
did it, that the roads, bridges, and
infrastructure provided the means or
the individual couldn't have done
it is shallow negative thinking in my
view, but many liberals think that
way.

That type of thinking places the cart
before the horse. Government is a
necessary parasite that every society
must have to provide internal and

external protection. In a free society government can't sustain itself or produce a profit, it survives only on what it takes in the form of profit from what always originates from some form of private business transaction, period.

Sure, the government got the roads, bridges, and infrastructure, but, where the hell you think government got the seized money from to do that? Not that I disagree, but it got the money out of the profit of many, many struggling small businesses.

All of this anti-business propaganda is just plain economic ignorance. They have no idea what made America the greatest and wealthiest nation in the history of mankind.

Without the millions upon millions of small private businesses out there making a profit there will be no profit for the government to take to provide anything for anyone, period.

Lord have mercy on our great nation,

with all of this negative anti-business propaganda thinking out there we are going to need it.
SIRMANS LOG: 20 AUGUST 2012, 1201 HOURS

IF THE REPUBLICAN DOESN'T WIN A POLITICAL TRIFECTA IN NOVEMBER IT WILL BE THEIR OWN FAULT!
I have pounded it to where I am almost blue in the face; conservatives limit your message to around three things. Sure, you respond to any and everything then its I stand by my earlier statement.

I know staying with so few things will bore the hell out of most people but that is what you want, that is proof they are not forgetting what you stand for.

The simple minded and many others will succumb to the course of least resistance and grab the democrat goodies that is why the default volt almost always goes to the democrats. And unless a conservative stand for lower taxes, more jobs, and strong national defense the default volt will carry the day in the general election most of the time.

In my view the problem with the republicans is they are out there attacking for blood and is acting and reacting all over the map and no one truly knows what they stand for. To hell with the other guy, the people want to know what about you, what are you gonna do, can I trust and depend on you.

The hard working independents and majority tax paying voters will never desert one who pounds to no end lower taxes, more jobs, and strong national defense. Yet, somewhere in the polling it got republicans running away from the three things I advocate especially lower taxes.

I say to hell with all of this polling go with your gut sometime, people want someone who is willing to go down with what they themselves believe in and what is right for America.

I will tell you now if you are afraid to pound away on lower taxes your chance of winning in November are going to be slim to none and that is nobodies fault but your own.
SIRMANS LOG: 14 AUGUST 2012, 0852 HOURS

The sad fact is THE WELFARE STATE can't be saved and anyone that thinks it can is in denial. I can dissect an economy as well as anyone and I'm telling you the days of the welfare state is over we are now living on borrowed time.

The republicans just as the democrats are dead set on saving the welfare state but I'm telling you the republicans will fail even worse than the dems simply because they think they can cut the growth of government, wrong.

It is impossible to reduce the growth of

government in this welfare state because there are too many social programs that will kick in and increase the dole side of government, thereby growing government in a reverse negative way. There is no need to add more details they can be found farther down in my writing.

All I will say at this time is we must start somewhere to prevent going back to the Stone Age. The first thing that must be done or nothing else matters anyway because holding on to the welfare state leads only back to the Stone Age.

The complete elimination of the minimum wage must be done now or it will be impossible for the USA government to survive, that is a fact, there is not a doubt in my super mind about that. You don't have to believe me just keep on living; the minimum wage must go, one way or another if we are to have any chance of survival as a nation.

I pound and pound this fact and still no

one wants to hear it but we all will sooner than we think. The elimination of the minimum wage will allow the American people to save themselves because soon the government is not going to have the money to do so.

The government doesn't generate any profit it is a necessary parasite and every penny it takes in comes from some form of private business profit. And in this anti-business atmosphere the shallow minded liberals are trying to make it impossible for a business to make a profit.

The liberal and masses of economically ignorant government dependents are biting the hand that feed them and the really sad part is they don't have a clue absent the bias predominant socialist/liberal news media. God I ask in your name, save the only home I know.
SIRMANS LOG: 12 AUGUST 2012, 0203 HOURS

ARE REPUBLICANS AFRAID TO

PROMOTE LOWER TAXES?

Folks, I am a self-made writer and a screwed up neurotic one at that.
But, one thing I am not is a phony hypocrite. I may not be a man of extra strong physical courage and feel overall I am too passive. Still, I think I am a man of conviction and I try to do my best in spite of my handicaps.

I said all of that to try to make a point, it is no wonder the survival of our freedom is under attack. I feel we may lose our freedom because fewer and fewer people are willing to standby their true convictions. Every politician seems to be putting a finger up into the wind by means
of political polling.

The republicans had a TRIFECTA in the bag, but, I feel they stand a
good chance of losing now simply because they are too afraid to stand up to their convictions. Instead they are putting all of their faith in all of this extreme polling; I hope they are right for the sake of the country

and our freedom.

I really don't have a favorite political party my only concern is who will best hold on to our dwindling supply of freedom. Even if the republicans do win the TRIFECTA it will only allow a little more time before nature's supreme law of "Natural selection" lowers the boom.

The republicans don't need to give out a lot of details all they need to do is just pound and pound to no end lower taxes, more jobs, and strong national defense and nothing else. But, I believe they are afraid to pound lower taxes, and what I say to that is when the majority of Americans don't want lower taxes the country is no long worth saving anyway.

If that is the case there soon won't be any freedom left to save. We will be a bankrupted welfare state headed back to the Stone Age. No matter what our beliefs are we all are Americans, you don't have to agree with anything I write, but thank God I

still have the freedom to say the things I write.
SIRMANS LOG: 30 JULY 2012, 1219 HOURS

A CONSERVATIVE WILL ALMOST ALWAYS LOSE THE GENERAL ELECTION BY CONSTANTLY ATTACKING!

Unless one has deep wisdom and perspective they won't understand why I'm so against all of this attacking. It is simply because it is a loser's strategy.

Today's voter has a short attention span and need to be constantly reminded of who you are and what you stand for. Sure, attacking the other guy tears him down, but that doesn't remind quick forgetting independents and the majority what you stand for.

Everyone already knows the sugar daddy/momma liberal is going to tax and spend and give away the store even when we can't afford it, especially women and African

Americans already know this, they just don't care.

It is like the warnings on a pack of cigarettes and all of the warnings against big juicy high fat burgers, etc. people already know the danger and choose high risk living, so preaching fire and brimstone on how bad someone or something is may work against a conservative but very little against a sugar daddy liberal giving out goodies. As long as the goodies keep coming they will say "I don't care if the canidate looks like ET as long he is nice to me."

Knowing better we all has a weakness to take the course of lease resistance and grab the goodies, but if a mature conservative step up and promise lower taxes, more jobs, and strong national defense he will win with the independents and majority tax paying public.

I'm telling you, in the general election you don't normally beat a liberal

by constantly attacking, Reagan didn't go that route nor did "W." Attacking in itself distracts from who you are and what you stand for, and in the final analysis that is the reason people vote, the individual
sometimes has little to do with it.

I would but there is no way in hell 90 percent plus African Americans
would vote for Herman Cain. He would be the best friend we ever had
but there is an indelible stamp on too many out there that says his way
of thinking is the enemy. Sure, some people will vote for you simply
because they hate the other guy so much, but in most cases it is going
to take a lot more than that to win.

So, those are the facts, it is what it is. It is what you are going to do that really matters and if conservatives are not going to stress lower taxes, more jobs, and strong national defense I don't believe we will get the trifecta in November. I certainly hope I'm wrong on this.
SIRMANS LOG: 18 JULY 2012, 1440

HOURS

I BELIEVE CONSERVATIVES HAS A SLIM TO NONE CHANCE OF WINNING THE BIG TRIFECTA IN NOVEMBER WITHOUT ADHERING TO MY ADVICE!
This is my advice to all conservatives or anyone with conservatives leaning; never stray from only three things, low taxes, more jobs, and strong national defense.

Sure, make just one statement on current events or what ever but then revert back to the three said priorities, period. The attack dog predominate socialist/liberal news media don't like you and is going to do everything in their power to defeat you. That said, as a rule the general public tends to be simple minded with short memories.

That means to win the big TRIFECTA conservatives must keep it simple with not more than the three priorities, low taxes, more jobs, and strong national defense only. Sure, doing that will bore the hell out of most people, but that is what you want up until the election that will be proof that they won't forget what you stand for.

Otherwise, off to the side stirring up controversial and everything else the independents and others attention span won't remember what the hell you stand for, then the liberal news media will rip you apart. No matter what the liberal news media propaganda attack machine says the independents and winning majority will remain faithful and loyal if you never depart from the three said priorities, they are your armor.

I'm telling every conservative or anyone with conservative leaning if you don't take my advice we have a slim to none chance of winning the big TRIFECTA in November. That is just the way it is. There are no absolute guarantees in life the most anyone can do is create the best conditions to win.

The liberal news media propaganda attack machine in my view is the biggest obstacle standing between a big TRIFECTA conservative win for the conservatives in November. All they know is to attack, attack, and attack, and it is futile to try to defend against their every barrage without armor.

The three said priorities is your armor only if you bore the hell out of people by sticking only with them. Sticking with them conservatives win, veering off them then the liberal news media propaganda attack machine will rip you apart and defeat you. God I ask in your name save our great nation.
SIRMANS LOG: 12 JULY 2012, 1227 HOURS

WHAT IS IT ABOUT THE MINIMUM WAGE THAT PEOPLE CAN'T UNDERSTAND?

Cutting the minimum wage is cold, wrong and a mistake, doing that will only aggravate and increase poor people's misery. No one has ever read or heard me encourage lowering the

minimum wage, if you thought you
did you weren't listening.

I have been drum beating it until I'm
almost blue in the face to "Get rid
of the minimum wage that is a world of
difference from lowering the
minimum wage. I am talking about
eliminating the minimum wage
entirely, period. That is the only things
that would bring back some
sanity to our economy, and is the only
thing that will save the USA with
freedom intact.

Otherwise, welfare states worldwide
will become dictatorships or some
other form of authoritarian rule within
five years just to keep order. What
people that lack perspective and a
basic understanding of economics fail
to realize is it is not the amount of
money that matters; it is the buying
power that truly counts.

Eliminating the minimum wage for the
whole nation would shift the
economy into a natural balance where
money would count for something, or

there would be no way to prevent bartering. The minimum wage is what allowed the welfare state a foot in the door, now the welfare state beast rules the roost.

A free market place economy is bases on the fact that any one can pay as much or less as he sees fit for a job so long as no one is forced to accept it, or even pay the help with commodities if no force is applied. Sure, what I just said was to the extreme, but, I am all about survival, and with the condition the USA is in financial, nothing should be ruled out.

In my humble opinion the only thing stopping the USA from becoming a dictatorship right now is the second amendment. However, after November all of that could drastically change, I think the hidden priority agenda will be to use some type of UN treaty to trump the second amendment and override the second amendment once and for all. That is my analysis.

The liberals are just waiting on their chance to pounce. I ask in your name, God save freedom in America. SIRMANS LOG: 10 JULY 2012, 1447 HOURS

NEGATIVE ADS WORK, SURE, WITH IGNORANT AND UNINFORMED PEOPLE.

I'm one that has never bought into this idea that negative ads always work. Sure, they work with the ignorant and uninformed but not everyone fits that description.

I hold to the rule that if you are a good and decent person and makes sure people know what you stand for then good and decent people will support you. In politics I think the dumbest thing one can do is exercise in futility by trying to defend against every bad or incorrect charge directed against you. At worst even if they brand you a SOB, what else is new, like Nixon said, sure, he is a SOB but he is our SOB.

As long as the conservatives keep
pounding low taxes, creating more
jobs, and strong national defense and
nothing else the independents
and vast majority won't care what the
bias socialist/liberal news media
propaganda attack machine brands
you. And they will prove it by
saying he is our SOB with their vote.

But, if the conservatives get side
tracked into shouting matches of he
said she said and every other kind of
juicy fodder it will be just what
the doctor ordered for the liberal
propaganda machine. Then with
phony polls and every other kind of
distortion one can imaging the
liberal propaganda attack machine will
rip you to threads and defeat you.
Staying with the three said things is
your armor, don't abandon them.
SIRMANS LOG: 4 JULY 2012, 1759
HOURS

**GET OVER IT CONSERVATIVES
OBAMACARE IS NOW THE LAW OF
THE LAND AND THAT IS A FACT!**

About this new Supreme Court ruling on Obamacare, I think some conservatives just ought to get over it, period. They should realize what the liberals have always known that the constitution means only what five people say it means.

From a political point of view you control the court with the legislative process by controlling who get on it, not by ranting on and on over spilled milk. Why do you think the die hard liberals always fight to the last man/woman over who gets on the court, wake up and wise up conservatives, it is all about control, not ranting.
SIRMANS LOG: 4 JULY 2012, 1045 HOURS

A BAD MARRIAGE!
I keep hearing market, market, and market to no end, and I'm sick and tired of it. That is the biggest problem with the USA and welfare states worldwide. The governments of local, state, and federal need to get the

hell out of the stock market and the stock market need to get the hell out of the government.

They are two different things and don't mix. All government spending especially on an individual basis must be kept separated from the free market place economy, period, or else. SIRMANS LOG: 20 JUNE 2012, 2024 HOURS

MY MINIMUM WAGE CRUSADE
One way or another the minimum wage is going to be completely eliminated. It boils down to how it gets done. At some point soon nature's Supreme law of "Natural selection" is going to do it for the USA and all welfare states world wide unless we act first.

Ever since the "New deal" we have let the liberals call the tune and give away the store now we have to pay the piper in blood, sweat, and tears, and even that may not be enough to save our nation.

There is no escaping our lack of judgment; it is a law of nature, there are no free rides. However, if the USA and the welfare states world wide go ahead and completely eliminate the minimum wage first modern civilization may be saved.

Otherwise, if nature's supreme law of "Natural selection" has to lower the boom then once the dominoes starts falling it may mean all the way back to the Stone Age. God, I ask in your name stay your hand!
SIRMANS LOG: 12 JUNE 2012, 1559 HOURS

"ANY NATION EMERGENCY SURVIVAL PLAN" BY FREDDIE L. SIRMANS, SR.
Folks, I am a self-made writer and I tell it as I see it, straight raw no chaser, right or wrong, believe it or not, take it or leave it is what you get from me.

Never mind the experts and learned

economist, I Freddie L. Sirmans, Sr. with my great supernatural wisdom is offering my "Any nation emergency survival plan." Its coming folks, a totally economic collapse, and I am offering my plan free to prevent total chaos that may lead back to the Stone Age.

No, I haven't lost my mind I have been writing basically the same thing for over twenty years, now. Here is the first thing that should be done now even before nature's supreme law of "Natural selection" lowers the boom.

Any nation that expects to survive when the boom is lowered and the domino's starts falling best take heed and act now because the whole thing may be like a fast moving tree top wild fire. Number one, the USA and all of the welfare state must completely get rid of the "Minimum wage" now, not tomorrow or when you get around to it.

That would set free the free market

place where it would function naturally like it is supposed to. Every business would still have to pay a higher wage to get the best workers.

But, free market means free without force, meaning if someone want to work for a dollar a day with room and board why shouldn't they have that right, because when this welfare state is flat broke and can't borrow another dine it may take something like that just to survive.

Number two, "All government free aid on an individual basis must be kept separated from the free market place national economy" because that is what causes consumer inflation and unreasonable prices. And the only way to keep free unearned government handout spending on an individual basis from subsiding price raising and contaminating the free market national economy is for government to use tokens or script and operate its own commissaries, housing, and clinics.

With unearned individual government

spending being kept separate and not subsiding price raising no merchant can charge more than the poor and working class can afford because of their number, there is never enough rich to support an economy.

This way the poor and working class will be able to buy the bare necessities of food and medical care, and those that falls through the crack will get tokens or script as to not freeze or starve. This economic survival plan is not perfect but it is sound and will prevent total chaos.

The welfare state has spoiled a lot of people and following this plan won't be easy and will cause much hardship and pain, but, almost anything is better than losing our freedom forever or mired in total chaos.

With the minimum wage gone people will be free to barter or do whatever it takes to survive because a broke government may be lucky just to provide national defense, internally and externally.

This country has never known anything but freedom, and I assure you without the minimum wage blocking self-help the people will barter and do whatever it take to legally save themselves and the nation.
SIRMANS LOG: 27 MAY 2012, 0042 HOURS
PS: As always I don't expect my great supernatural wisdom to be taken seriously but positive human effort is never wasted.

HE/SHE IS OUR SOB!
One thing about Nixon is in private he was known for very colorful language. In one case one of his aides was branded on and on how bad he was. I'm paraphrasing Nixon's reply: "Sure, he is a SOB, but he is our SOB."

So, the message here to all conservatives is: The socialist/liberal news media propaganda attack machine is definitely going to brand from bottom to top anyone with any conservative leaning a SOB.

But, the fact is as long as one keep pounding until the cows come home lower taxes, more jobs, and strong national defense that will be their armor plated protection.

Then no matter what they are labeled or branded there will still be more than enough freedom loving Americans to carry the day, and say he is our SOB with their vote.
SIRMANS LOG: 22 MAY 2012, 1222 HOURS

ADD ON INJECTION: 22 MAY 2012, 2118 HOURS

It is impossible to save a country or its economy when its government prevents big business failures. That prevents any way to get rid of waste, decay, and inefficiency. Doing that put's the whole country at risk by weighing down and crowding out positive new growth until a collapse is unavoidable.

Nature's supreme law of "Natural selection" doesn't hit any one on the head with a hammer, but nothing escapes it effect. "You can't get blood out of a turnip" for a simple reason, there is none there. It's the same with a broke government, soon its not going to take care of the elderly or anyone simply because there will be no money there.

The welfare state days are over and anyone disagreeing is simply economically ignorant and in a state of denial. Business profit is government's only means of support directly or indirectly, but by government promoting waste, decay, and inefficiency unabated soon it will be impossible for businesses to make a profit.

Knowing businesses can't make a profit won't stop government from draining the last one dry. The reason is government sees itself as the great lord and master super social and family provider, plus the fear factor lets the politician know the masses will be coming with the pitch forks when no more government hand outs are forth coming.

Still, nothing is written in stone man still has the power to choose his destiny.

With all of these polls and figures flying around now-a-days I never forget, "Figures don't lie, but liars sure can figure."
ADD ON INJECTION END

WILL CIVILIZATION RETURN TO THE STONE AGE?

In life with few exceptions the rule is: "No guts no glory, no risk no gain." There is a simple reason why it is impossible for an economy to work properly when government is too involved. Government acts against the laws of nature, and especially natures' supreme law of "Natural selection."

It's very simple; government stops and prevents the elimination of waste, decay, and inefficiency. You can't have life, growth, or lasting progress being bogged down with waste, decay, and inefficiency. You see, government doesn't adhere to supply and demand; it operates only on force and power.

Whereas, a free market place economy with unrestrictive competition will supply far more than any nation can use or demand. Believe it or not, the main reason why is it does something a pure communist or socialist system will never do.

Free competition is the stick to get rid of inefficiency, and allowing an unlimited individual reward motivates the most power energy packed force in our entire human makeup, that energy force is greed.

People without wisdom and perspective will never understand this but there is no other force in our human makeup with enough motivation to produce more jobs, food, and everything else than any one nation can use.

Sure, like electricity greed is very dangerous, but free competition bridles it without forceful eliminating or shutting it down completely like communism and socialism does. We use to have this great freedom in the USA, but with the "New deal" and our welfare state we are well on our way to being a communist or socialist state.

It is simple; there has never been and never will be a rich and wealthy country with job for almost everyone without a lot of greedy rich and wealthy entrepreneurs to make it happen. Rich people are not the same as poor people with money, there is a world of difference in attitude.

People naturally have different talents and abilities and should always have the same opportunity, but to always receive the same result in life (reward) is stupid and against the laws of nature. But, generally that is what a communist and socialist state promotes.

That is why government should never be heavily involved in the operations of private businesses. Government is always going to reward its friend and punish its perceived enemies. In a democracy governments job is to collect only enough taxes to protect the nation and the upkeep of the infrastructure, period.

It is not government's duty to be a social and family provider from cradle to grave. In my view government as a social and family provider is like eating your seed corn or even more horrible eating your young.

Before the "New deal" government acting as a nanny state had never been done on a mass scale in the history of mankind. It destroys a nation's culture, nuclear and extended family system, and any emergency capacity to barter.

That is a total destruction of the foundation for human survival; western civilization has little left of

those 5,000 year pillars of support.
When we fall no one knows where it
will end, the Stone Age is not an
impossibility.

Still, with my great wisdom and insight
I'm seen as a nut case, fool, and
a throwback to the eighteenth century
that don't know what the hell I'm
talking about. The only thing I can say
about that is: I pray to God you are
right and I'm wrong. God bless the
USA.
SIRMANS LOG: 15 MAY 2012, 1051
HOURS

JUST LIBERAL PROPAGANDA BACKGROUND NOISE!

There has never been and never will be
a pure communist or socialist state
that could feed its entire people home
grown without natural resources to
sell. So, to all of these economic
ignorant people that hate capitalism,
rich people, and big business, be
careful of what you wish for because
unless drastic changes are made you
are going to get it.

Unless my deep wisdom advice is taken which the egg heads will never do means your wish will be granted sooner than you think. The reason is freedom and democracy demands responsibility, accountability, and people with sound judgment, which fewer and fewer has in this great nation today.

Soon when the boom is finally lowered there will only be two choices left, total chaos or total authority, history has shown there will be no compromised middle ground.

Damn, nobody is listening, my God; this dumb idea that one has to refute every single little charge against you in a political race is just plain nonsense. I don't think, in fact I know you can't make hateful negative people like you no matter what you do.

I am a firm believer that if one dwell on doing what he feel is fair and right people of decency and goodwill will accept you for who you are and what you stand for. But, to deny and be overly concerned about every little negative charge by liberals that only want to destroy you is an exercise in futility.

People don't love you because you are perfect people love you because you are human caring and decent. People got eyes, they can see unfairness from the liberal propaganda attack machine, and they will ignore it if the intended victim will ignore it.

It will be just like water off a ducks back if one ignores it and keep pounding low taxes, more jobs, and strong national defense. Otherwise, if the intended victim can't ignore it then the people can't ignore it either and will detect weakness, which is not good.

Just make only one statement to any new charge and get back to pounding and pounding your message.

Like Nixon said, "The haters can't

destroy you unless you hate them back, then you destroy yourself." This lean and mean liberal news media propaganda attack machine takes no conservative political prisoners.

That is just the way it is in this knockout drag out battle for this nations survival as a free nation. This is it folks, this is for all the marbles, there will be no tomorrow for individual freedom in this great nation.

I'm in the fray folks, I don't want to be, but this is my beloved home the only home I know. So be it, destiny is calling on my great wisdom and perspective.
SIRMANS LOG: 10 MAY 2012, 2359 HOURS

A WELFARE STATE IS LIKE AN INCESTUOUS RELATIONSHIP!

Economically wise a welfare state may be compared to an incestuous relationship. In a normal free market place economy private enterprise generate the profit with little to no government interference.

Through taxing the government takes off the top only a small cut needed to protect the nation and maintain the infrastructure. That way the economic process and everything else functions normally.

Nature's supreme law of "Natural selection" keeps all prices under control by maintaining a balance between the merchant and the consumer. But, in life there is always going to be people that fall through the cracks like the poor and disadvantage.

Throughout history until the "New deal" came along the nuclear and extended family system, the church, and community organizations aided these people. It was not a perfect system but it was the best system known to man for well over six thousand years.

Just like life itself it had a rebirth and death cycle known as booms and busts. Then, here comes liberal do-gooder geniuses that think they can take all of the risk out of life. Life can't exist without risk because there must be someway to get rid of waste, decay, and inefficiency. They didn't realize that nature's supreme law of "Natural selection" is based on a survival need for anything to exist over time.

Now, we as a nation are putting all of our faith in and depending on one super sugar daddy provider government from cradle to grave to survive. Thereby taking away a survival need for a system that has been around well over six thousand years, how dumb can we get?

More and more there is no survival need for the once strong nuclear and extended family, or to have good morals and values, that is why they are slowly ceasing out of existence. There is no wonder why men are marring men and women are marring women.

I could go on and on for hours on the damage the welfare state has done to our economy, our morals, our values, and everything else we use to hold dear. But I will end by saying: I believe we as a nation are sc...... ourselves incestuously. Great solution to the problem is found throughout my writing and books, Freddie L. Sirmans, Sr.
SIRMANS LOG: 09 MAY 2012, 1208 HOURS

GOVERNMENT INDIVIDUAL SPENDING MUST BE KEPT SEPARATE FROM THE NATION'S ECONOMY IF IT IS TO BE SAVED.

The reason I pound so hard for government to separate all of its individual spending and get the hell completely out of the nation's free market place is because that is the main thing killing our economy.

The stock market and all of that other

stuff is just side issues.
Government involvement is what's killing the economy that is why I stress so hard that government must start using tokens or script when aiding the poor and disadvantage on an individual basis.

That will prevent government spending from contaminating the national economy. Sure, we must not let people freeze and starve but the only way government can aid the poor and disadvantage without destroying the free market place economy is by operating its own commissaries, housing, and clinics system with the use of tokens or script to keep that spending separate.

The destructive system we are using now takes tax money from one group of Americans, and then in competition against we the tax payers gives that money to another less producing group which results in higher and higher prices and taxes on everyone.

That is why tokens or script must be used for all government spending that is done on an individual basis, that would keep merchants from raising prices higher and higher on everyone, which is the reason for the consumer inflation we have today.

The main way this contamination occurs is when government gives out masses amounts of money on an individual basis. That infusion of mass amount of unearned (government spending is unearned spending) money allows merchant to raising prices higher and higher against ourselves we the tax payers.

The government subsides price raising on everyone by giving out masses amount of money and food stamps to the poor and disadvantage on an individual basis, there is not enough rich and others to support too high prices.

Without that government subsidy to the poor and disadvantage, basic food and medical prices could never go

higher than the poor could
afford.

So, instead of subsiding higher prices
on everyone in helping the poor, the
poor and disadvantage can still be
helped without the government
driving up prices, if only government
would use tokens or script in its
own government operated support
systems.

Making the government use tokens of
script for all individual government
spending would stop this nonsense, as
you see, economic ignorance is staring
us in the face.

So, in closing this chapter, I repeat, for
this nation and our economy to
survive all government spending done
on an individual basis tokens or script
must be used, period. God! I ask in
you name, save our great nation.
SIRMANS LOG: 08 MAY 2012, 0958
HOURS

CAUTION! CONSERVATIVES THINK

BEFORE YOU LEAP!
Warning! Stop! Don't! For now don't
cut or reduce spending or anything
else. It will only reduce the size of the
pie and make everything worse
and maybe even instantly wreck the
economy.

A smaller pie means fewer jobs and
everything else, and it may even
double the dole population and push
the debt from 16 trillion to 32
trillion. Government spending ain't the
problem it is how it is doing the
spending.

It shouldn't but if government is going
to do social and provider spending
anyway it should be done by providing
government commissaries,
government housing, and government
clinic with the use of tokens or script.

Government get the hell out of private
enterprise and let private enterprise
and the free market place sink or swim
on its own, this is an order. To kick
start and get this whole process rolling
right now eliminate the minimum

wage.

The welfare state era is over.
Government in the role of social and
family provider has out lived its time.
Profit from American businesses
is the only thing that supports our
government either from directly
taxing business or indirectly from the
wages paid to business employees and
their property.

Let's describe business profit as your
seed corn. When government is small
and taking care of only national
defense and infrastructure like parks,
roads, and bridges it only needs to
take a small amount of business seed
corn profit. That way the business will
have plenty left to raise and grow
another bumper crop.

But, when government takes on a
social and family provider role it
rapidly grows government demanding
it take bigger and bigger chunks
of businesses seed corn profit. The
bigger chunk government takes the
less seed corn the business will have to

grow another crop.

Our government welfare state as social and family provider now has grown so large there is not enough business seed corn profit available for the welfare state to take to survive without killing off American business. That is what this liberal created social and family provider government has brought this great nation too.

There is no foreign invader, we are now face to face with the enemy, and it is economic ignorance. We are now at economic death door, we no longer have a choice, we either separate all government spending from our free enterprise economic system or the economy will definitely collapse and freedom in this nation will be lost forever.

This can be done by the government not giving anyone money unless they work for the government, also no food stamps. Of course the government must help people and not let people freeze or starve. But, government must do that by operating government run commissaries, housing, and clinics with the use of tokens or script, but there must be a separation, otherwise it will be impossible for our less than free market place economy to survive. Also, we must as a nation eliminates the minimum wage, that way the people can save themselves.

It coming folks, this government is broke and the sooner that sinks in the better. Right now to the masses of government dependents that kind of talk about economic failure is just pesky noise. Lord save this great nation. Folks, I know my drum beat to eliminate the minimum wage don't seem to make sense, but I have the wisdom and perspective to know it is the only way out.

A minimum wage is a forced manipulation of the free market which means we don't have a free market place economy. If we did we wouldn't be in the sad shape we are in. Without a forced minimum wage the whole economy would be in balance.

With no minimum wage labor and cost would balance each other allowing the very poor to afford and pay their own food and medical bills, which now is impossible. The minimum wage ain't free, people don't realize it but it just forces a business to charge more for everything you buy.

Sure, in moderation a higher wage is not a bad thing, but when has a government handout ever stopped with moderation. Besides, it is done by force and that is totally against the rules of a free market place economy.
SIRMANS LOG: 7 MAY 2012, 1527 HOURS

QUICK WORD OF KNOWLEDGE INJECTION:
Economically speaking caring for the poor or anybody must be kept separated for a free market place to work, that is the problem now, you can't have unlimited individual

government spending standing between the merchants and the consumers and expect a healthy sound free market place economy.

What you will have is uncontrolled consumer inflation like what is taking place now, that and the "Minimum wage" is the fuel that is spinning consumer inflation out of control.

There is no way in the hell to stop this economy from expanding beyond control and collapse from it own weight with the course it is on. You don't have to take my advice; the wait won't be very much longer.

Government must sell off damn near everything and give up its social and family provider role, period. Will it happen, no? If the USA government doesn't eliminate the "Minimum wage and give
up its social and family provider role will the USA economy survive, no.
So, what is going to happen to this great land of the free and home of the brave, you really don't want to

know the answer to that as I see it.

Well, if you insist and won't take no for an answer I guess I have no choice but to tell you what I think is going to happen. I believe to buy time and avoid biting the dust our Welfare State and the Federal Reserve as co conspirators will finish selling off what is left of our freedom and sovereignty to some foreign highest bidder like a cheap street walker. And we will end up as debt slaves.

So, how you like me now?
SIRMANS LOG: Last update 27 MARCH 2012, 1613 HOURS

THE END

**BY FREDDIE L. SIRMANS, SR.
WEBSITE: www.FLSirmans.com
BLOG:http://www.freddiesirmans
word.com**

www.ingramcontent.com/pod-product-compliance
Lightning Source LLC
Chambersburg PA
CBHW051456170526
45166CB00001B/273